Theories
Of the Fable
In the
Eighteenth Century

Thomas Noel

Columbia University Press
New York and London 1975

The Andrew W. Mellon Foundation, through a special
grant, has assisted the Press in publishing this volume.

Library of Congress Cataloging in Publication Data

Noel, Thomas, 1940–
  Theories of the fable in the eighteenth century.

  Bibliography: p.
  1. Fables—History and criticism.   I. Title.
PN980.N6   809   74-23251
ISBN 0-231-03858-5

To Bobita

A fable in herself: she dances, barks, sings, flaps
her flippers, and always stands out.

Acknowledgments

My thanks to Gene Mohr, who proofread and found it thoroughly fascinating; to Bonnie Díaz, who typed and found it mostly legible; and to Barrilito, who smoothed out the whole project.

The material in this volume was originally submitted to the University of Illinois as the thesis for the doctoral degree in Comparative Literature.

University of Puerto Rico   THOMAS NOEL
June, 1975

Theories of the Fable
In the Eighteenth Century

CHAPTER ONE

The Popularity of the Fable and the Rationale

Since the term "fable" carries with it a considerable number of references and connotations, it seems best to clarify the matter at the beginning. In addition to the animal or Aesopian fable, the term has been used to designate literary plot, story, or narrative in general. Loosely used, it also suggests the fairy tale, the fabliau, the animal epic, or any narrative form that employs non-human characters or results in a moral lesson.

This study concerns itself with the first mentioned, the short didactic narrative, commonly employing animal characters, also known as the animal fable, the Aesopian fable, or the apologue. This definition of "fable" is probably the one most commonly accepted by the average person in the twentieth century. Even though the form has long since faded from the active literary scene, certain fables—the one about the fox and the grapes, for example—still inevitably find their way into the process of elementary education. Certain collections, particularly the fables attributed to the legendary Greek sage Aesop, continue to hold their own on the list of recommended children's literature. Everyone knows the formula—pithy narrative using animals to act out human foibles and consequent moral, either explicit or implicit—and most people remain familiar with a handful of traditional fables, even though that familiarity might be hidden away in the dim recesses of the mind along with other pre-puberty remembrances.

In the twentieth century the humble fable has virtually no literary status. One finds scholarly articles on Aesop in journals devoted to classical literature and an occasional literary-historical study of the form; but contemporary opinion, especially in the English-speaking world, generally regards the fable as a type of children's literature. There are exceptions, such as James Thurber's *Fables for Our Time*. Much of Thurber's success, however, derives from the reader's delight at finding sophisticated plots and heavily ironic morals in a form typically associated with children's bedtime stories. The attitude varies somewhat in France, where the seventeenth-century fabulist Jean de La Fontaine still merits a niche in the literary hall of fame; but no contemporary first-rate French poet would devote himself exclusively to the fable, generally considered even more out-dated than the epic as far as serious literature is concerned. Twentieth-century French and German critics do tend to grant the fable more literary prestige than their colleagues of the English-speaking world, but even in the continental countries the prevailing attitude would probably relegate it to children's literature.

The numerous learned discussions of two centuries ago, as well as the hundreds of volumes of printed fables, attest to the interest in and respect for the genre at that time. Indeed, the eighteenth century seems to be the only period in which the fable has been considered a legitimate literary genre. In addition to an impressive assemblage of "full-time" fabulists, most neoclassic poets and other writers include among their collected works a few fables, although perhaps now tucked away among the "juvenilia" or "scraps and fragments." Most of these fabulists, moreover, aimed at the general public, not just children; those who did limit themselves to a juvenile audience are offset by the many who directed their fables to mature readers.

Much of this eighteenth-century output consists of repeated translations and revisions of the traditional fables associated with Aesop and passed on through Phaedrus and other Latin fabulists. Multiple volumes published as "The Fables of Aesop" or "The Fables of Phaedrus" demonstrate that originality was not the compiler's aim. With the victory of the Moderns in the "battle of the books" early in numerous continental imitations of the English models. The German "moralische Wochenschriften" provide an excellent example of the rapid rise of interest in fables. Early volumes contain few or none; they begin to appear regularly in the late 1720's and become an anticipated feature in the succeeding years.[4] By the 1740's the trend culminates in *Der deutsche Aesop,* a weekly devoted exclusively to fables. Literary journals conscientiously reviewed volumes of fables, as well as making them a standard feature; and in some cases the reviews ran to article length. Translations, which introduced the more successful fabulists into other countries, merited the same critical attention.

There had been earlier periods of intensified interest in the genre, times when readers and critics considered Aesop one of the wisest of the Ancients and when poets produced original fables. Tradition claims that in his own time Aesop, although a slave, was respected as a sage of the first order. Plato regarded poetry as detrimental to the public good and would have banned all forms from his republic except the fable, which he considered morally beneficial. Notable eruptions of fable writing occurred in the late Middle Ages and again in the sixteenth century. The last three quarters of the eighteenth century, nevertheless, seem to be the only period in which the fable has ever been considered a fully qualified literary genre. People not only composed fables in this epoch but ranked them as serious literature, attaching no restrictions such as "children's literature" or "folk literature"; and they granted to the fabulist all the rights and distinctions of poet. In France and Germany the fable invariably received detailed treatment in works on theory or principles of literature, treatises on *belles-lettres,* and encyclopedias of the arts. The considerable deference accorded it, however, does not imply that it ever achieved equality with epic or tragic poetry, an estimation that even the most zealous fabulists would find ridiculous. Although unequivocally established among the standard literary genres, it was distinctly a minor genre. The Englishman Robert Dodsley, who wrote fables and an essay on the genre, unreservedly qualifies the fabulist as poet and creator but then proceeds to temper the estimation: "I rank him not . . . with the writers of epic or

dramatic poems; but the maker of pins and needles is as much an artist, as an anchorsmith: and a painter in miniature may show as much
skill as he who paints in the largest proportions.'' [5] Depiction of the
anchorsmith as artist perhaps overextends the credible limits of art, but
despite the dubious metaphor Dodsley puts the fable in a critical perspective characteristic of the times.

   Neoclassicists typically respected the unchallengeable supremacy
of the epic among the literary genres, an esteem which sometimes
resulted in a rather frantic urge to create modern epics on a par with
those of the classical world. If the aspiring poet doubted his ability to
work on the magnitude of Homer, however, he could respectably
dedicate modest talents to the Aesopian fable. Both genres, moreover,
belonged on the same scale, the epic at the higher, more sublime end
of it and the fable at the lower, humbler end. The influential French
critic and literary theoretician Le Bossu formulates this relationship in
his treatise on the epic, and it underlies numerous eighteenth-century
definitions of the fable. It establishes the fable as a legitimate member
of the family of literary genres—perhaps the runt of the family but
well connected in his relationship to his big brother the epic.

   This study undertakes to trace the course of this fable phenome-
non, beginning with the upsurge of interest in the latter half of the seventeenth century and then focusing on the various discussions of the
genre produced during the eighteenth century in the English, French,
German, and Spanish languages. The emphasis is on theories of the
fable formulated during the period, a good many of which exist, since
the orderly, analytical eighteenth-century mind was even more fond of
theory than it was of the fable. No attempt is made to provide an
esthetic treatment of individual fables or fabulists or methodically to
review critical opinions of the time as applied to specific fables or
collections. The different aspects frequently tend to intertwine, however. Theoreticians commonly use critical perceptions into the work of
Aesop, La Fontaine, or some other fabulist as a framework on which
to formulate their own theories. Moreover, most writers who composed fable theories also composed fables; and it is by no means rare

to find their ideas expounded in fables especially invented or adapted for the purpose. This practice results in fables about how to write fables, often with the major ''dos and don'ts'' summarized in moral tags.[6]

Certain historical trends help to explain the suitability of the fable for prevailing eighteenth-century tastes and aims. The most prominent of these was growing social concern, particularly as it aroused interest in education. Common opinion considered moral instruction the paramount pedagogical obligation and expected literature to assist in discharging it. A firm underlying moral, therefore, was required of all literature, which, as a result, tended to become didactically oriented. The fable, didactic by definition, fulfilled this requirement more neatly and naturally than any other genre: it falls short of being a fable if its ''literary'' part does not culminate in moral instruction. Many commentators, especially early in the century, claimed that a fable or any other literary piece lacking a salient moral lesson could not even be classified as literature.

Increasing interest in the fable accompanied widespread degeneration of schools and pervasive decline of trust in them. The movement for educational reform which flourished in the sixteenth and early seventeenth centuries had floundered and largely disintegrated. Originally reform-minded Protestant schools had lost their progressive momentum and contented themselves with instilling simple piety, while in the Catholic world the Jesuit institutions, which a century prior Francis Bacon had eulogized as the best in existence, continued to grind Latin grammar and rhetoric into their pupils and to ignore the scientific and other innovating currents reshaping the universe. Universities everywhere were mostly anachronisms. Some had advanced so far as to incorporate sixteenth-century innovations into their structures and curricula, but many still clung to medieval scholasticism.

Under these circumstances people understandably tended to lose faith in institutionalized education. In *Some Thoughts Concerning Education* (1693) John Locke readily acknowledges advantages deriving from classroom instruction but concludes that the disadvantages, such as the immorality invariably acquired by boys grouped together under inadequate supervision, outweigh them. He recommends a private tutor, as does Rousseau in *Émile* (1762). The obvious drawback is the forbidding cost, which the rising, newly literate middle class could not afford. As a result of distrust in the established schools and the impossible expense of tutors, education frequently became a family matter, the father or mother undertaking to give the lessons. Professional schoolmasters had long employed fables as an educational tool; but as a result of the shift to parental teaching, many collections in the eighteenth century aim specifically to assist the layman in educating his children.

Further in *Some Thoughts Concerning Education* Locke adamantly declares moral instruction to be the overriding purpose: "It is virtue then, direct virtue, which is the hard and valuable part to be aimed at in education. . . . All the other considerations and accomplishments should give way, and be postponed, to this." [7] In teaching children to read he vigorously recommends fables, the implicit morality of which concomitantly achieves his aim of imparting virtue. He specifies that the instructor should approach reading casually, arousing the child's own interest in learning. Coercion should be avoided at all costs. Once interest has been aroused, the teacher's next step is selection of a suitable book, ". . . wherein the entertainment that he finds might draw him on, and reward his pains in reading; and get not such as should fill his head with perfectly useless trumpery; or lay the principles of vice and folly. To this purpose I think Aesop's Fables the best, which being stories apt to delight and entertain a child, may yet afford useful reflections to a grown man; and if his memory retain them all his life after, he will not repent to find them there, amongst his manly thoughts and serious business" (p. 113). At another point Locke refers to Aesop's fables as "the only book almost I know fit for children" (p. 152).

Locke also recommends fables for teaching languages, especially Latin. He resolutely opposes the traditional pedagogical practice of

requiring vast amounts of memorization, and his efforts to eliminate
the endless hours spent learning grammar and rules derive from the
same source. The student laboriously masters such mechanics, which
fade from his memory and serve no purpose whatsoever once the language has been learned. Convinced that grammar can be avoided,
Locke suggests a bilingual, interlineal edition of Aesop's fables, a proposal which he himself subsequently brought to fruition: *Aesop's Fables, In English and Latin, Interlineary, For the Benefit of Those who
not having a Master, would learn either of those Tongues.*[8] In the
preface he further explains the purpose of the volume in facilitating
mastery of English or Latin, as the case might be, without first having
to absorb rules of grammar.

Locke's *Thoughts* met with enthusiastic reception not only in England but also on the Continent: a French translation appeared in 1695
and a German version in 1708. The work was published soon after his
Essay on Human Understanding—1690 and 1693—and it supplements
the earlier, more famous tract. Among other outlets, Locke's educational concepts were disseminated by the moral weeklies which
flourished during the first half of the eighteenth century in all German
cities; and apparently they inspired the prominent philosopher Christian Wolff, whose pedagogical ideas parallel Locke's, even though he
does not mention his English predecessor.[9] Wolff also recommends
the fable as the supremely effective method of inculcating moral
truths.[10]

The pedagogical notions of the French churchman Fénelon resemble Locke's both in their impact and their progressive air. Fénelon also
vigorously recommends fables, and he composed a volume of them
which was originally intended to instruct his pupil, the young Duke of
Burgundy, but which was translated and widely adopted elsewhere.[11]
His *Traité de l'education des filles* [12] is remarkable in that it even discusses the matter at a time when females were usually taught no more
than the necessary social graces and the intricacies of managing a
household. Fénelon, to be sure, does not undertake to create the enlightened woman: the sections of the *Traité* concerned specifically

with female education frequently decree what *not* to teach. About two thirds of the work, moreover, discusses instruction of children of either sex.

Parallel to Locke, Fénelon declares the inseparability of moral and intellectual education and opposes forcing children to learn: it is far preferable to avoid severity, to keep the lessons informal, and to feed the child's natural curiosity. To teach reading he suggests that the teacher make a game of it—and play it in the child's native language. Fénelon roundly denounces the common practice of compelling children to undertake Latin before familiarizing them with the written vernacular. To inspire reading interest as well as to initiate the entire educational program, he proposes that the teacher capitalize on the child's love of stories. Tell him a "clever and harmless" story,[13] particularly one about animals, which invariably attract his attention. But he warns against introducing girls to heathen mythology, which is "impure and full of absurd blasphemies." After telling the story or fable, the teacher should wait and allow the child's curiosity to grow to the point where he begs to hear another. After this process has been repeated once or twice, curiosity will induce him to open the book of fables himself. Since Fénelon is first and foremost a churchman, however, his ultimate goal is to guide the child to the Scriptures. He admonishes against forcing the Bible on him but regards stories and fables, although instructive in themselves, important primarily as a means of leading him willingly to the Scriptures. The teacher accomplishes the transition by first introducing his pupil to Biblical stories and narratives. Once he has thus acquired familiarity with the Bible, the reading program leads beyond stories into the more didactic and abstract sections. Fénelon disapproves of literature for its own sake or as entertainment, especially for women, claiming that it introduces notions far removed from reality and virtue. For much the same reason he denies women the Spanish and Italian languages: knowledge of them allows easier access to dangerous books.

Despite the emphasis both Locke and Fénelon place on the use of fables in elementary education, the eighteenth century did not limit the genre to young minds. Its very acceptance as a literary genre stemmed from the conviction that everyone could read fables for edification and enjoyment. The cultured father could delight his children with Aesop before sending them to bed, but he could unabashedly read fables for his own entertainment too. Besides attracting people of all ages, the fable reached all social classes, an advantage remarked time and again; no other literary genre could speak both to the king and to the peasant. It provided moral instruction in a way understandable and palatable for everyone, avoiding the resistance that direct lessons arouse. "An agreeable lesson," poet and critic Christian Gellert calls it; [14] and most eighteenth-century discussions of the fable express the same sentiment.

Gellert also stresses that the fable contributes to the moral development of the *masses*. The notion of "speaking to the masses" became crucial as the century progressed and the revolutionary currents grew into waves. The comfortable goal of molding a moral citizenry often tended to be replaced by the revolutionary aim of arousing the citizenry to create a new society. As a result, numerous fables which appeared later in the century substituted social protest for the traditional moral didacticism. Karl Emmerich describes the fable as first-rate *Tendenzdichtung* (poetry with a purpose), [15] declaring that it prospered as the "predominant literary genre of the learned Enlightenment. . . . The bourgeois poets saw in its allegorical and didactic nature the best method to popularize new moral views, ethics, and principles of living, which were opposed to those of the courtly society" (p. 5). No longer simply the medium for moral enlightenment, the fable now focused on social criticism and became a weapon for use in the class warfare dominating the period. Emmerich's Marxist viewpoint becomes apparent even before the unmistakable "class-warfare" confirms it. In any case, his relegation of the fable entirely to *Tendenzliteratur* is an overstatement of the situation. Even the didactic-minded eighteenth century meant literature to be enjoyed; and much of the extensive fable writing, even the best, was accomplished with no more than a polite bow to didactic purpose. The intentions of the fabulist might be satirical, even flippant; but he still attaches a moral tag because the formula requires it. However, in its broad outlines the trend which Emmerich remarks is valid. Others have noted it too. A pair of contemporary Spanish fable collectors, for example, assert in the commentary to their anthology that the fable developed in two fundamental ways during the eighteenth century: it rose in prestige until ranking among the literary genres, and it became a vehicle for social protest, permeated with the revolutionary spirit of the times.[16]

The controversial notion of animal mechanism, deriving primarily from Descartes and eliciting heated arguments pro and con for more than a century thereafter, seems to have little direct bearing on the increasing interest in fables. It is, however, of peripheral significance, at least insofar as that the prominent fabulist Jean de La Fontaine pointedly controverted the materialistic concept and suggested the service of his fables to teach about animals and to delineate the bonds between men and animals.

In "Discours à Madame de la Sablière" La Fontaine adamantly rejects the Cartesian beast machine. He declares that animals not only possess souls but also *think,* even though *reflection* exceeds their capabilities. The distinction between thought and reflection is narrow but decisive; the latter supposes the powers of memory and forethought, which men possess but which animals lack. Bestial thought is thus limited to the immediate situation. Animal and human mental capabilities differ in depth, however, not in kind. La Fontaine also declares this proximity of man and animal in the preface to his first published collection of fables (1668), in which he maintains that their purpose is to assist in the formation of judgment and morals, especially in children, as well as to impart knowledge, specifically of the characters and properties of animals. Understanding of animals, he points out, advances understanding of oneself, since man "summarizes" all the good and bad in brute creatures.

La Fontaine's defense of animal intelligence does not mean that he wrote fables in order to crusade for bestial rights and dignity. On the contrary, the matter probably had little to do with his becoming a fabulist. The defense of animal souls by him and others seems to stem from a general concern for spirituality in the face of the rising materialism of the time. Beasts, it was argued, have souls because they are creatures of God. But if one perceives a divine spirit in animals, why not in all the multiple aspects of the universe? This pantheistic possibility is realized, at least to an extent, late in the eighteenth century by Johann Gottfried von Herder. Herder, as we shall see later, regards the fable as an expression of the primeval unity of man and all nature. Modern man contends with a fragmented universe, he claims; but his primitive ancestor keenly felt himself to be an integral part of a unified whole. The fable derives from this early "golden age."

Throughout the eighteenth century, to sum up the foregoing, the fable was highly regarded as either a literary genre with educational utility or an educational tool with the inherent attractiveness of literature; and since moral didacticism was expected of all literature, the difference between these two viewpoints is negligible. The social or "revolutionary" fable followed later in the century and represents an extension of the original didactic fable. It endured approximately as long as did enthusiasm for the Revolution.

Toward the end of the eighteenth century the fable itself—in its personification of animals and physical objects—evokes interpretation as an expression of natural unity. According to this interpretation, propounded by Herder and others, the genre originated in the distant past before man cut himself off from nature and structured his life on artificialities. At this "Garden of Eden" stage men and animals could communicate, and there was nothing strange about seeking wisdom from the examples of beasts. "Follow nature" had always been one of the commandments leveled at aspiring fabulists, admonishing them to adhere to observable rational order; but in the late eighteenth-century trend toward Romanticism *nature* becomes *Nature,* and "Follow Nature" harks back to a primal Golden Age of spiritual unity and assumes prophetic overtones. Dominated by this interpretation positing a primitive, popular origin, the fable merges into the general body of folklore revered and collected by the Romantics, experiencing occasional revivals as a form of nature poetry.

At the same time, the fable wore itself out as a workable literary genre. Heavy practice during the century rapidly exhausted its limited possibilities for variation, resulting in endless repetitions of the same old material. By the early nineteenth century commentators were sounding a pessimistic note about the futility of producing more fables. In the sense that an art form lives only so long as it presents possibilities for creative innovation, however, the fable was dead long before the death knell was sounded.

In addition to the foregoing explanations for the popularity of the fable, it must also be admitted that the genre makes relatively few demands. Any would-be writer or moralist could try his hand at it without suffering pangs of inadequacy. Simplicity and brevity are paramount virtues in the fable, qualities which also permit the literary dilettante to dash off a specimen without being wearied by prolonged creative thought. The genre demands neither subtlety, nor philosophical profundity, nor poetical lyricism. All of these qualities, as a matter of fact, were often criticized as detrimental to its basic aim and style. Simplicity and moral purpose, as construed by the amateur, frequently resulted in smug morality, absence of any artistic touches whatsoever, and monotonous repetition of multiple existing fables. In the hierarchy of fabulists which the orderly neoclassic mind devised, Aesop, La Fontaine, and Phaedrus occupied top positions and offered the most promising examples to follow. By the time interest in the genre waned, the vast amount of fable writing had not diminished the lustre of the top of the hierarchy, while the majority of those comprising the lower ranks had been forgotten.

CHAPTER TWO

La Fontaine and the
Seventeenth-Century Forerunners

It would be a gross error to label revolutionary Locke and Féne-lon's mere advocacy of fables in education. Their enlightened peda-gogical approaches and their methods of employing the genre to arouse interest in reading and learning represent innovations; but fables themselves had been long familiar to every schoolboy, particu-larly from his Latin lessons. A 1657 collection with English and Latin texts on facing pages includes an explanatory note on the title page: "Every one whereof is divided into its distinct period, marked with Figures; so that little Children being used to write and translate them, may not only more exactly understand all the Rules of Grammar but also learn to imitate the right Composition of Words." [1] Far from en-joying the fables, harassed schoolchildren would tend to associate them with the ordeal of Latin grammar and composition. We can see why Locke tried to avoid grammar altogether. Sir Roger L'Estrange echoes Locke's criticism in the preface to his 1692 collection of fables when he complains of the common Latin schoolbook, "This Rhapsody of Fables is a Book Universally Read and Taught in All our Schools; but almost at such a rate as we Teach Pyes and Parrots, that Pronounce the Words without so much as Guessing at the Meaning of them." [2] Claiming that the moral becomes irretrievably lost during the mindless rote recitation, L'Estrange aims for a workable English translation in which the child will comprehend both fable and moral.

In his vigorous, colorful style L'Estrange also upholds the genre against scorners who consider it fit only for women and children, equivalent to "the Fooleries of so many Old Wives Tales." [3] These disparagers, declares L'Estrange, are the kind of people dissatisfied with anything not "Unsociably Soure, Ill Natur'd, and Troublesome; Men that make it the Mark as well as the Prerogative of a Philosopher, to be Magisterial, and Churlish." To judge from his style, L'Estrange does not seem one to be easily intimidated. Yet he feels obliged to defend the fable and, therefore, himself for dealing with it. Apparently many of his contemporaries and predecessors disparaged it as a childish trifle. Indeed, there is every reason to believe that the disparaging estimation predominated in the seventeenth century. Whatever its value as a pedagogical tool, reigning opinion accorded the fable slight literary worth.

Earlier, in 1651, John Ogilby went so far as to attach a prefatory apology to his English version of Aesop, published subsequent to his translation of Virgil: "If any . . . shall accuse my Judgement, and Choice, who had the Honour of Conversation with *Virgil,* that I have descended to Aesop, whose Apologs this day are read and familiar with Children in their first Schools . . . the Dictates of my reason denie I should make Answer to such men . . ." [4] But he makes his answer, nevertheless, claiming that Aesop has received high esteem even in the most learned times and has always been studied to great advantage. Not content with his own humble apology, Ogilby also solicited dedications from James Shirley and William D'Avenant, both of whom sing the praises of Aesop and of Ogilby's translation.

Jean de La Fontaine's twelve books of fables appeared at intervals between 1668 and 1694. In his prefatory comments La Fontaine refrains from overt apology for dealing with the fable, but his discussion is low-keyed and even deprecatory in regard to his own efforts. He excuses his use of verse by noting that Socrates reputedly spent his last hours versifying Aesop and that Phaedrus composed poetic fables. La Fontaine considers his own work to be translations of Phaedrus but emphasizes that he has translated only a selection, leaving others for future fabulists in the event that interest in the genre should grow.

Originality does not concern La Fontaine, so that later critics who censure his lack of it reproach his failure in something never attempted. The French fabulist implies the existence of a static body of fables— that associated with the name of Aesop—which has been inherited and reworked by Phaedrus and other fabulists. To write fables thus means to translate and adapt from this existing body. An *original* fable would not be an *Aesopian* fable.

La Fontaine belittles his own talents. He humbly asserts that Phaedrus' elegance and admirable brevity far surpass his own ability and that his modest contribution mainly has been to "brighten up" the fables. Although claiming no originality, he knows that he cannot merely rewrite a well-known collection of fables and expect applause for his efforts. His own productions therefore include an element of novelty in addition to the touch of "gaiety." [5] La Fontaine clarifies that gaiety does not suppose excitement of laughter but a certain charm that can be given to even the most serious subjects. And then he hastily affirms that utility, the moral and educational purpose, of course predominates; and this affirmation introduces his discussion of the instructive value of the fable, mentioned in the previous chapter.[6]

La Fontaine sometimes uses the term "apologue" more or less interchangeably with "fable." At certain critical points, however, he distinguishes between them, such as when he defines the two components of the *apologue*, "of which one can be called the body, the other the soul. The body is the fable; the soul, the moral." "Fable" in this sense denotes the story or narrative. La Fontaine also introduces the term "parable," which further confuses the issue: "we see that the truth has spoken to men by means of parable; and what is a parable but an apologue, that is to say, a fabulous example?" [7] Later analytically-minded critics, who exercise great care in differentiating between such terms as "fable" and "parable," would be shocked at La Fontaine's nonchalant interchanging of them.

Throughout the seventeenth and eighteenth centuries "apologue" designates the *Aesopian* fable, as does the word "fable" by itself, when used in its narrower sense. But "fable" also has a broader meaning, referring to *plot* or *narrative*. J. Baudoin prefaced his 1669 *Les Fables d'Esope Phrygien* with an essay "To the Reader, on the Subject of Fables," in which he defines the fable: "An artifice, which by some likeness represents the truth." [8] He then proceeds to list the various kinds, depending primarily on the class of characters employed—human, animal, supernatural. Baudoin's categorization, a standard one, uses "fable" to refer to literary narrative in general. The apologue or Aesopian fable falls into the category of *fable propre,* which uses the example of beasts and inanimate things to demonstrate a lesson.

Baudoin proceeds to enumerate various sources for fables, such as the imagination and external nature; and his treatise still concerns the broad application of the term "fable." He specifies that all fables belong to poetry and not to philosophy: philosophers adhere strictly to the truth of things, whereas poets lead us there by way of certain agreeable detours. Fables, nevertheless, must convey truth and morality, failing which Baudoin would join Plato in banning them along with other forms of poetry. Despite this admonition, however, he avers that he could cite multiple examples of their beneficial use by the Ancients for moral edification.

Antoine Furetière, friend and follower of La Fontaine, makes clear in a foreword "To the Reader" in his *Fables morales et nouvelles* (1671) that the volume contains "Fables commonly designated Aesopian." [9] He declares that the unique advantage of the genre derives from its flexibility: it instructs the people equally as well as kings. Dramatic poets, for example, lack a single form able to reach all classes of people: they compose tragedies in order to instruct "the Heroes" and comedies to teach the common people. Furetière then catalogues other advantages of the fable, most of which will be repeated time and again during the next hundred years. Its inoffensiveness merits his special attention and is also the characteristic which succeeding fabulists most often point out to their readers. The argument goes like this: we rebel against preaching and indeed take umbrage at any suggestion of reprimand or even advice. Preachers and moralists being fellow human beings subject to our own weaknesses, we easily conclude that they do their job out of pride, dislike, or envy. As a result, we ignore the lesson or criticism and scrutinize the teacher in order to discern reciprocal faults and weaknesses in him. When animals act out the lesson, it is imparted "free of passion and interest." We are confounded to observe animals, guided only by their natural instincts, conducting themselves better than we ourselves behave aided by the power of reason. The examples of animals consequently reprove and correct much more effectively than the preaching of members of our own species. Considering the eminent advantages of the genre, Furetière expresses his surprise that so few modern writers have exploited it. He praises Aesop and Phaedrus, especially the latter, and wonders at the virtual omission of the two sages from the venerable body of Ancients emulated by Moderns. There exist many translations, among which La Fontaine's ranks as the most outstanding; but nobody, he declares, has *imitated* them with notable success. Furetière thus proposes inventing original fables, rather than simply reworking the traditional ones.

Furetière's enthusiasm for the fable apparently was not shared by Nicolas Boileau-Despréaux, in his time the most influential champion of classical literary standards. In his *L'Art poëtique* (1674), frequently consulted as the bible of poetical propriety, Boileau employs the term "fable" only in its broad application as literary plot or narrative. Nor does he even mention the Aesopian fable or La Fontaine, evidently considering the form insignificant. René Le Bossu's *Traité du poëme epique* (1675), a treatise with a rigid enough classical orientation to merit Boileau's praise, also discusses "fable" in the sense of narrative or plot. But in addition Le Bossu takes up the Aesopian fable and establishes a relation between it and the epic which reappears in numerous subsequent treatments of the fable, most notably La Motte's.

Le Bossu begins by distinguishing between the ancient and modern mentalities, characterizing the latter as comparatively simple and direct. When the ancients expressed themselves, however, "the truth ordinarily was disguised under those ingenious inventions which for their excellence bear the name Fables.'' [10] It is interesting that Le Bossu associates fables, which include myths, legends, and narratives, with the Ancients, implying the unnaturalness of the fictive method for the modern mind. He later proffers a comprehensive definition of the fable: "a discourse invented in order to form the morals by means of instructions disguised under the allegories of an action" (p. 12). It consists of two parts, the truth and the fiction, the former being concealed but forming the foundation. The first step in constructing a fable is selection of the truth; only after completing this initial step does the fabulist contemplate the second, which is reduction of the truth to an action or depiction of it in an illustrative story. There are, finally, three kinds of fables, differentiated according to the characters introduced into the narrative. The *Raisonnables* cast men and gods as actors; the *Moratae,* animals with certain superimposed human attributes; the *Mixtes,* a combination of the other two (p. 21).

The epic, belonging to the first classification, *concerns* history and philosophy but *is* both poetry and fable. The fable constitutes its substance, while poetry determines the manner of presenting it. Le Bossu's definition of epic thus conforms to his definition of fable in general but is distinguished by the poetic qualification "narrated in verse in a probable, entertaining, and marvellous manner" (pp. 9–10). A fable, however, is a fable, whatever its ultimate generic affiliation. Aside from the names accorded the characters, he points out, there is no difference between the epic fable and the Aesopian fable. To express the relationship in another way, the difference between the two genres emerges only upon denomination of characters. Le Bossu illustrates his logic by comparing the *Iliad* with a fable of Aesop's: "It is of little importance for the nature of the fable whether one selects names of beasts or of men. Homer chose the latter. . . . Aesop, in his own way, gave animal names to all. . . . Homer's fable is 'raisonnable', and Aesop's is not; but that does not mean that the one is more or less fable than the other" (p. 35). Aesop also utilizes gods and men, he further notes, while Homer occasionally imbues animals with the power of speech.

Since Le Bossu's argument endows the Aesopian fable with independent status, it is not surprising that later fabulists and theoreticians should avail themselves of his ideas. Subsequent commentators frequently distort his comparison, however, most typically by claiming, supposedly on Le Bossu's authority, that length constitutes the sole difference between the Aesopian fable and the epic. Yet Le Bossu clearly differentiates on the basis of character, not length; furthermore, he compares Aesopian fable and epic *fable,* not epic. The fable underlies the epic; but poetry, the other component, determines the manner of presentation. The poetic component represents an enormous variable; on it depends whether the basic fable flowers into an epic or remains restricted to more modest proportions.

Fable in the broad sense of plot, story, or tale—any kind of narrative or sequence of events—also describes John Dryden's *Fables, Ancient and Modern* (1700), which includes verse translations from Homer, Ovid, Boccaccio, and Chaucer and a selection of original poems. Fables of the Aesopian variety play no part. Dryden, however, would apparently have disagreed with Le Bossu's assertion that all fables contain an edifying truth; he admits familiarity with immoral, or at least amoral, ones. In the preface he piously declares his attempt in this collection to "chuse such Fables, both Ancient and Modern, as contain in each of them some instructional Moral," [11] and offers his regrets for not always having taken such judicious care in earlier works. He explains, perhaps somewhat wistfully, that had not this instructional aim been his guide he would have selected from Chaucer such tales as the Miller's and the Wife of Bath's. Dryden uses "fable" and "tale" interchangeably. In *The Hind and the Panther* (1687) he further confuses terminology by equating "fable" with "episode," declaring in the preface that the work contains "two *Episodes,* or Fables, which are interwoven with the main Design." [12]

The *Fables* of Fénelon also exemplify the broad connotation of the term, although every selection included by this clergyman is irreproachably committed to moral instruction. The volume comprises a mixture of Aesopian fables and oriental tales. Eustache Le Noble's inclusion of both terms in the title of his *Contes et fables* (1697) seems redundant; the sequence in the volume suggests a random pattern, such as Conte i, Conte ii, Fable iii, Conte iv. All are versified, terminate with moral tags, and employ both human and animal characters.[13]

John Dennis, a classically-oriented critic whose literary observations span more than twenty years, considers fable to be plot; and in the "Preface" to *Iphigenia* (1700) he declares it to be the key component of a piece of literature: "I consider, that the Writing of good Verses may make a man a good Versifyer, but 'tis the forming of a fable alone, that can make a Poet." [14] The fable consists of moral and action, but the former takes precedence: "the very first thing that he who makes a Fable does, is to fix upon his Moral. A Poetical Fable is compos'd of one action and a moral. The Action the Body of it, and the Moral the Soul." [15] Both the division and the metaphor are familiar by now. In "The Stage Defended" (1726) Dennis compares the Aesopian with the dramatic fable: ". . . every true Dramatick Poem is a Fable as much as any one of Aesop's; it has in its Nature a direct Tendency to teach moral Virtue, and can therefore never be contrary to a Christian Temper & Spirit . . ." [16] Every "true" drama, whether tragedy or comedy, is a moralizing fable. Dennis makes the assertion airtight by withholding "trueness" from any production without conspicuous moral purpose, implying that such material even fails to qualify as literature. Dennis also defines fable in words reminiscent of Le Bossu: "For a Fable is a Discourse most aptly contrived to form the Manners of Men by Instructions disguised under the Allegory of an Action." He further emphasizes moral preponderance by asserting that drama, far from a diversion, is "a philosophical and moral Lecture." At this point Dennis' conception of a theatrical production resembles a dramatized sermon.

Aroused by Sir Richard Blackmore's claim that invention or selection of an epic plot precedes specification of the moral—based on the assumption that a moral can be drawn from any narrative—Dennis adamantly defends the opposite order in a letter to Sir Richard: "Can anyone believe, that Aesop first told a Story of a Cock and a Bull, and afterwards made a Moral to it? Or is it reasonable to believe that he made his moral first, and afterwards to prove it, contriv'd his Fable? Now I know of no difference that there is, between one of Aesop's Fables, and the Fable of an Epick Poem, as to their Natures, tho there be many and great ones, as to their Circumstances. 'Tis impossible for a Poet to form any Fable, unless the moral be first in his Head.'' [17] Dennis distinguishes between the *nature* of the fable, wherein Aesopian and epic are identical, and the *circumstances,* comparable to Le Bossu's *poetry,* wherein they differ widely. Dennis's formulation, however, seems far-fetched. It is plausible to depict Aesop with a moral in mind, inventing a little tale to illustrate it; but there is something ridiculous in the notion that Homer created or adapted the extended adventures of Odysseus simply to exemplify a moral lesson. Later critics, such as Marmontel, justifiably reject the feasibility of such an orderly, compatible relationship between the epic and the Aesopian fable.

Dennis also avers that an epic must end happily, at least for the principal characters: a tragic ending would destroy "all Poetical Justice, and consequently, all Instruction: Such a Poem can have no Moral, and consequently no Fable, no just and regular Poetical Action, but must be a vain Fiction and an empty Amusement." [18] Considering all the innocent animals that get eaten up in Aesop's fables, we must assume that Dennis abandons, at this point, the comparison of epic and Aesopian fables.

In addition to narrative or plot, many writers also construe "fable" as designating classical myths and legends, or any pagan mythology. Bernard Le Bovier de Fontenelle's *De l'Origine des fables* (1724), for example, traces the origins of classical mythology to superstition and ignorance, implying that similar explanations account for the development of Christianity. Antoine Banier intends no such iconoclastic implications in his *Le Mythologie et les fables, expliquées par l'histoire,* in which "fable" refers to the stories and legends that comprise classical mythology. [19] He includes *fables morales* as one kind, noting that they typically permit animals the power of speech "in order to teach man his duties or to criticize his defects." [20] The Aesopian fable, according to Banier, thus appertains to classical mythology. Pierre Bayle's *Dictionnaire historique et critique* (1697) also favors the classical meaning: a fable is a legend or a mythological story. Aesop's is just one kind, which Bayle also designates "apologue."

"Fable" thus encompasses an extensive literary and mythological territory. Seventeenth-century and early eighteenth-century writers dealing with the *Aesopian* fable take care to define their reference, typically by occasional substitution of "apologue" or by adjoining Aesop's name. Later in the eighteenth century, however, "fable" comes to denote exclusively the Aesopian fable. Other terms, such as *"conte," "Erzählung," "novel,"* and *"roman,"* acquire currency and affix themselves to other categories of narratives. As early as 1719 La Motte prefaced his *Fables nouvelles* with a "Discourse on the Fable," under which title he launches a discussion of the Aesopian fable, evidently certain that his readers will understand his reference. Later in the century Jean Le Rond d'Alembert marks the distinction between *"conte," "fable,"* and *"roman."* All three designate fictitious stories, but notable differences separate them: the *"fable"* is "a narrative in which the aim is moral, in which falsity is often perceptible, like when animals or trees talk." The *"conte"* constitutes a short realistic fiction or a fable "without moral aim." *"Roman"* simply designates a long *"conte."* D'Alembert admits that *"fable"* occasionally refers to other narratives too.[21] In his *Dictionary of the English Language* (1755), Samuel Johnson's primary definition of "fable" is "a feigned story intended to enforce some moral precept," which he illustrates with a quotation from Addison referring to the Aesopian fable. Later fabulists interchange "fable" and "apologue," although the latter term is less common in England and rarely used in Germany. In the early nineteenth century Antoine Arnault asserts that in French "fable" and "apologue" are synonyms.[22] Nowadays the word "apologue" is little known, and "fable" has lost the meaning that linked it to classical mythology. It still denotes a fictional narra-

CHAPTER THREE

Aesop as a Popular Figure and the Fable in England

Boileau, as remarked earlier, does not discuss the fable in *L'Art poëtique*, nor does he mention La Fontaine. The omissions are, in a way, surprising, considering that La Fontaine's fables had been published and well received only a few years prior and that Boileau was apparently acquainted with La Fontaine personally and poetically. His failure to treat the genre becomes understandable, on the other hand, when one takes into account the prevailing low opinion of it at the time. In the seventeenth century the fable typically ranked as no more than light verse or children's literature, hopefully edifying, but not worth discussion or definition. Whatever Boileau thought of La Fontaine as a poet, he undoubtedly scorned the genre in which the fabulist had chosen to work. It should also be kept in mind that La Fontaine regarded his own fables as little more than translations of Phaedrus.

Nor had the fable made its way into literary society by the time Bayle published his dictionary (1697). Bayle expounds on "fable" in general and cites Aesop's as one kind; but he includes no article under "apologue," mentioning the term only in a footnote to the entry "Aesop"—which in itself is brief. The Aesop of fable fame remains undistinguished, moreover, among several men of the same name who lived in ancient times.

Although the Aesopian fable had not yet gained admission to formal literature, Aesop himself was beginning to acquire renown in the latter years of the seventeenth century. Among other public appearances he played a modest part in the Ancients-Moderns controversy which intermittently dominated the European literary stage at this time. One of the *Nouveaux Dialogues des morts* (1683) of Fontenelle, a leading spokesman for the Modernists, transpires between Aesop and Homer. The former questions the latter about the *"grands mystères"* [1] which worshipful readers perceive in his works. In reply, Homer himself ridicules this semi-religious veneration of his epics, claiming that he never intended any such profundity.

Sir William Temple, in "An Essay on Ancient and Modern Learning," defends the Ancients against this and other onslaughts of Fontenelle, the indefatigable champion of the Moderns. After first declaring the overall superiority of the Ancients in learning, Sir William turns to poetry and draws the same conclusion "in Favour of the Ancients, that the oldest Books we have, are still in their kind the best." He singles out Aesop's fables and Phalaris's epistles as the oldest known prose works: "the first has been agreed by all Ages since, for the greatest Master in his kind, and all others of that sort, have been but imitations of his Original." [2] In retrospect Sir William should have confined himself to eulogizing the learning and literary superiority of the Ancients and should not have stressed the antiquity of these two works. His praise of Phalaris's *Epistles* inspired Dean Aldrich of Oxford to have a new edition prepared, which resulted in the scholarly row between Charles Boyle, whom Aldrich commissioned to edit the work, and Dr. Richard Bentley. In 1697 appeared Dr. Bentley's *Dissertation Upon the Epistles of Phalaris, Themistocles, Socrates, Euripides, and upon the Fables of Aesop,* in which the principal objective is to demolish the authenticity of Phalaris's letters. In a concluding chapter Dr. Bentley also refutes the authenticity of Aesop's fables, claiming that the Greek fabulist probably bequeathed no written works at all. Those which circulate under his name were collected and transcribed from an oral tradition at a later date, by which time they had so degenerated that we know only "the last and the worst." [3]

Jonathan Swift's *Battle of the Books* also began circulating in

manuscript form about 1697 at the height of the controversy rising
from Bentley's *Dissertation,* although the manuscript did not see publication until 1704. In it Swift includes the fable of the spider and the
bee. The spider, resembling a feudal lord, accuses the bee of being a
vagabond, continually buzzing from one source to another, never
drawing upon his own resources. The bee, in reply, questions at length
the proclaimed virtues of the spider and finally denounces him for,
among other things, narrow-mindedness and overbearing pride: cling-
ing immovably to his tiny realm of a few inches around, he ignores
whatever lies beyond its restricted boundaries. Aesop, intervening at
this point, settles the dispute between the two arguing insects in favor
of the bee. Ostensibly, therefore, the victory goes to the Ancients; but
Swift concentrates on illuminating the silliness of the entire squabble
rather than on awarding anyone a decisive victory. Interest in the controversy tended to diminish in succeeding years, partially owing to
Swift's satire. All such matters are difficult to take seriously once
laughed at.[4]

Concurrently with his participation in the Ancients-Moderns controversy, Aesop also enjoyed considerable success on the stage. Edme
Boursault's *Les Fables d'Esope, comédie,* a play starring Aesop, was
staged and printed in France in 1690. The fabulist represents wisdom,
virtue, and admirable simplicity; fables comprise a considerable portion of his lines. The melodramatic plot discovers Aesop, traditionally
deformed and ugly, enamored of a young maiden, who, in turn, respects but does not love him. The fabulist wisely and nobly surrenders
all claims to her. The popular appeal of the play apparently derived
largely from Aesop himself as a symbol of reason and wisdom and
from the numerous fables which he recites. Author Boursault remarks
on the success of his play in a preface to the printed edition and
proceeds to answer criticisms of it. One reviewer objected to the venerable Greek in a contemporary setting; Boursault maintains the universality of Aesop and the qualities he represents: Aesop was one of
the most reasonable men of the world, and reason is of all countries
and all times.[5] Boursault similarly parries charges of not having fol-

lowed the rules of dramatic poetry: one must make allowances for a character of such universal magnitude. He also pays homage to La Fontaine by admitting the inferiority of his own fables to his predecessor's. The play aroused sufficient enthusiasm among theatergoers to inspire Boursault to a second Aesop-drama, but *Esope à la cour, co-médie heroique* was not staged until 1701, a year after the author's death. In this second play Aesop exhibits his wisdom in the role of minister of state to Cresus, King of Sicily; but the elevation in rank does not alter his homely habit of advising through the medium of fables. The plot is a tangled affair involving marriage between two warring kingdoms, but Aesop eventually manages to unravel all the strands and restore the order of wisdom and reason.

Boursault's *Les Fables d'Esope* was translated into English by John Vanbrugh and staged in London.[6] The translator altered the play to the point of mutilation, however, apparently to suit prevailing London tastes. The result is a bawdy comedy. Aesop resembles the old fool more than the timeless sage; and the January–May aspect of his infatuation with the young girl—a cheeky wench—becomes a primary source of ribald humor. Aesop, moreover, reveals a penchant for off-color fables.

French writer Eustache Le Noble produced an Aesop-drama titled simply *Esope* [7] in which the Greek fabulist once again denotes wisdom, reason, and classical serenity. He manipulates two troublesome marriages, serves as arbiter of good taste in poetry, and, inevitably, wraps his wisdom in the guise of fables. In order that the production may conclude with a burst of spectacle, Aesop is made to command his animals on to the stage to sing and dance the praises of the king. Le Noble also published the collection *Contes et fables* mentioned earlier, and further fables are scattered throughout his miscellaneous works. Aesop himself appears repeatedly in his *Dialogues,* sometimes as one of the featured speakers—for example, in the third of ''L'Esprit d'Esope, Dialogues'' [8]—at other times merely to illustrate a point by means of an occasional fable. The dialogues involve a variety of personages—mythological, classical, allegorical, and contemporary—but the majority focus on the current political situation. In the third dialogue of "L'Esprit d'Esope," for example, Aesop advises a contemporary statesman on how to manage the turbulent world of Louis XIV.

Political and social fables abound from about 1690 through the early years of the next century. The anonymous *Esope en belle humeur,* printed in Amsterdam in 1690, teems with contemporary references, although the general tone, as the title indicates, is light. In the preface Aesop himself is made to solicit a new edition of his fables. Baudoin, author of the 1669 collection discussed in the previous chapter, objects, apparently satisfied with his own version; but he is scornfully silenced. Aesop considers justified, however, a request that selected fables by Furetière and La Fontaine be included in the new edition. The venerable sage then delivers an advertisement for the Amsterdam printer of the volume.

The two-volume collection *Fables Moral and Political,* purportedly translated from the Dutch of a certain Johan de Witt, appeared in London in 1703. It has a decidedly more sober air and purpose than its Amsterdam brother described above. A preface of essay length sets forth familiar edificatory purposes and advantages: fables instruct circuitously, thereby avoiding the resentment that unadorned precepts inevitably arouse. Everyone proclaims aspirations to virtue, but no one—especially "Great Lords and Princes"—willingly accepts instruction from another person. People soon forget principles and maxims, in any case, unless they are accompanied by "some Figures or Imaginations," [9] which fix them in the memory. Thus, fables and similar instructive narratives were invented. It is essential, however, that the fable speak intelligently to lords and princes at the same time that it speaks understandably to common men: "That the Nature and Essence of all Fables consists in this; That they relate things wholly incredible, by putting Words in the Mouths of Beasts, and making Plants, and other mute and speechless Creatures speak: What they are made to say, nevertheless, ought not to exceed the Capacity of Men of common Understanding; but the whole Fable ought to be related in such common and general circumstances, that every Reader may readily make the Comparison between those Images and himself, or other Men.'' No one, whatever his rank or education, should suspect that the fable aims to instruct or reprimand him, the slightest hint of which would arouse his immediate resentment.

The author grants the reader liberty to interpret as he will the fables in this volume but then in effect withdraws this liberty by asserting their political message: monarchical tyranny threatens to enslave Europe, and "all the liberal Arts and Sciences, all Virtue, and the Liberties and Properties of Men" face extinction. The menacing tyrant is Louis XIV. Far from the frivolity of *Esope en belle humeur,* these fables exude the anxiety of a nation facing engulfment by the Sun King. Sample fable: A Frenchman and a Dutchman are shipwrecked on an island ruled by a savage despot who demands that the two castaways renounce all liberties and previous allegiances and bow down as his minions. The Frenchman immediately acquiesces and begins servilely to flatter the despot. The Dutchman holds firm to his principles and is promptly murdered. In the grasp of a tyrant the honest, straightforward man perishes while the flatterer thrives.

A fable-craze, or perhaps more accurately an Aesop-craze, sprang up in England during the waning years of the seventeenth century and resulted in a sporadic series of six-penny pamphlets typically incorporating the name Aesop into the title. Mostly anonymous, all contain fables dealing with contemporary matters, many with the turmoil caused by Louis XIV's ambitions on the continent or the current Jacobite scare. Others, which are virtually scandal sheets in fable form, gossip about English society and provide a medium for contemporary wits to exchange naughty comments and polished phrases. In 1698, for example, there was *Aesop at Epsom: Or a few Select Fables in Verse;* also *Aesop at Bathe,* "by a Person of Quality," a selection of verse fables, mainly anti-Jacobite. Next in the succession of itinerant works came *Aesop at Tunbridge,* "by No Person of Quality" who claims to have discovered the fables along a road. *Aesop Return'd from Tunbridge* commits the road-weary wanderer to Bedlam, driven out of his wits either by the Tunbridge waters or by Tunbridge society.

Old Aesop at White-Hall, Giving Advice to the Young Aesops at Tunbridge and Bathe—"by a Person of What Quality you Please"—contains political fables. Finally, *Aesop at Amsterdam, Balancing the Aesops at Tunbridge, Bathe, Whitehal, and C.*, which commences with an "Epistle Dedicatory" to old Aesop, lately so widely traveled and prolific: "Father, Where the Devil have you been all this while? . . . Good Dad! don't come too near me, you stink most damnably of Sulphur, I'm almost suffocated. . . . What Country you have been in I can't tell, but by your new Fables I find that you have liv'd under a Monarchical Government, and you are mightily in love with it, as are my two elder Brothers of *Tunbridg* and *Bathe.*" [10]

Aesop continues his rambles in the ensuing years. The itinerary for 1699 includes *Aesop from Islington,* the preface of which remarks on Aesop's current habit of taking the waters. The author specifies, moreover, that his fables come from the East, not Greece, and submits his opinion of the Grecians, commonly credited with invention of the fable: "For it is no news to the Learned World, that these Grecians we so much admire, (for what reasons let Schoolmasters tell you, for I can't) were but wretched Filchers, and worse disguisers of the Eastern Wisdom, and patch'd up their *Aesop* from an Eastern Sage." [11] Aesop thus escapes from Bedlam and the monarchical sulfurs of hell only to be snubbed as a nonentity or one of a team of plagiarizers. The 1701 leg of the journey includes *Aesop in Spain,* which claims to be translated from Spanish and which is generally more solemn and political, as are *Aesop at Court* (1702) and *Aesop the Wanderer* (1704). All three reflect the war then being fought on the Continent. In later years, however, the lighter vein returns with such trifles as *Aesop at the Bear-Garden* (1715), intended as a parody of Pope. By the time of *Aesop in Masquerade* (1718) the Aesop pamphlets had run their course, except for a few stragglers—and the price had risen from sixpence to a shilling.

One of the "Aesop-at" group, *Aesop at Paris* (1701), was purportedly authored by Bernard Mandeville, the Dutch-born physician who achieved a contemporary fame or notoriety with his iconoclastic

The Fable of the Bees. The pamphlet alternates letters from Aesop to various personages with fables, all focused on the current political crisis soon to explode into war on the Continent. In 1705 Mandeville published a slender volume of fables entitled *Aesop Dress'd,* which he describes as written "after the Familiar Way of a Great Man in France, *Monsieur de la Fontaine.*" [12] These translations figure among the earliest introductions of La Fontaine into England. Mandeville also inserts a couple of his own fables into the volume but belittles them, nor does he evince any esteem for the genre at large. He remarks first on his original creations:

. . . but I am so far from loving them the better, that I think they are the worst in the Pack: And therefore in good Manners to my self I conceal their Names. Find 'em out, & welcome. I could wish to have furnish'd you with something more worthy your precious time: But as you'll find nothing very In-structive, so there's little to puzzle your brain. Besides, I desire every Body to read 'em at the same Hours I writ 'em, that's when I had nothing else to do. If any like these Trifles, perhaps I may go on; if not, you shall be troubled with no more of 'em.

"The Grumbling Hive," which Mandeville later developed into *The Fable of the Bees,* appeared the same year. It would be interesting to know Mandeville's original intentions with the work. Perhaps "The Grumbling Hive" was also a playful product of idle hours, but one which grew into an extended economic theory at a later date.

In addition to the "Aesop-at" series, other assorted satirical and polemical fables appeared in England during the early years of the eighteenth century. Swift, for example, produced several of this kind between the years 1712 and 1728, aside from the earlier fable of the spider and the bee. There were, however, English fabulists and moral-ists concerned with the genre as a means of instruction. Sir Roger L'Estrange's 1692 collection passed through several editions and was still being printed well into the next century. L'Estrange emphasizes the suitability of his fables for children, who are extremely receptive to impressions: "Children are but Blank Paper, ready Indifferently for any Impression, Good or Bad." [13] Education makes the man; and

L'Estrange suggests that the educational process is a race to fill the child with good before the bad has a chance to creep in. Fables help to win the race by making moral lessons "Gilt and Sweeten'd," since children are invariably attracted to stories. L'Estrange stresses that one should never allow children to learn anything "but what they may be the Better for All their Lives after"; and learning, for children, encompasses everything seen and heard. All people, however—not merely children—receive their deepest impressions "under the cover of some Allegory or Riddle" and comprehend "the Truth and Reason of Things, through the Medium of Images and Shadows." Images touch people more profoundly than reasons, which explains the antiquity of fables and parables as teaching devices.

L'Estrange disparages all English collections of fables prior to his own, claiming that some presume excessively on poetic license while others illustrate "Insipid and Flat" morals or employ "Coarse & Uncouth" styles so that they tend to harm rather than edify. Each one of L'Estrange's own fables, all in prose, terminates with a short moral followed by a "Reflexion," which combines the tone of a sermon with a length typically greater than both fable and moral. To the twentieth-century reader the pious verbosity of L'Estrange's fables is disappointing after the virile straightforwardness of the preface.[14]

Edmund Arwaker published his own collection of fables, *Truth in Fiction: or Morality in Masquerade* (1708), although he makes a conspicuous bow toward L'Estrange and claims "implicit Faith in that Worthy Gentleman's Performance." [15] L'Estrange, however, produced in prose, while Arwaker takes pride in his verse and declares that the versification in itself justifies the new edition. He then confesses to not having read L'Estrange's fables and to having purposefully ignored them in order to avoid charges of plagiarism.

The intensity of Arwaker's defense of the fable indicates his awareness of the scant or tarnished literary reputation of the genre, which the spate of sixpenny Aesop pamphlets certainly had not enhanced. Arwaker admits, "I am sensible, that, with some, the very Name of *Fables,* is enough to bring any Work, to which it is prefix'd, into Contempt, as a thing of no Use or Value; or at best, but a Child-ish Entertainment; and to render it as despicable and ridiculous as the Person of *Aesop* was, which appeared so very Deformed and Mean." He deplores this mistaken, although apparently widespread, notion that fables are merely "insipid Tales, composd to please children, and make Fools laugh" (p. ii) and extols the genre as a valuable medium to convey truth. Since few men can bear to contemplate truth "in its full Splendour," they must "by a pleasing Fable . . . be led insensi-bly to the Wisdom of an instructing Moral" (pp. ii–iii). Arwaker points triumphantly to Biblical utilization of fables, declaring that such an authoritative example should in itself confound all derogatory opin-ions.

For children the fable "gilds the Pill . . . they swallow the harsh Moral in the Diverting Apologue" (p. vii). The familiar ring of the statement arouses suspicion that Arwaker perused at least the preface to L'Estrange's fables, although both the sentiment and the metaphor can be found elsewhere. But Arwaker declares that the fable also in-structs adults, for whom it serves little purpose to provide a fellow man, no matter how estimable, as an example to be imitated: "they wou'd pretend want of Qualification, and desire to be excus'd: For, tho most Men are ambitious to ape, if not exceed their Superiors in Wealth and Vanity; they can contentedly give them the Preference in Virtue, and let them practise it without Emulation" (p. viii). The example of "Irrational Animals," however, allows them no excuse.

Arwaker stresses the pedagogical mission of fables but also boasts of the steps taken to make *his* agreeable. Verse both augments the entertainment and facilitates memorization. He claims to have in-fused all possible satire for further diversion and to have included four fables entirely of his own invention which the reader can amuse him-self by attempting to discover. Either his self-confidence withers or underlying cynicism surfaces, however, when he expresses his hope that "the World is not altogether out of conceit with musty Morals." But if this be the case, "I desire the sheets may not be put to the indecent Use, to which Waste-Paper is too frequently condemned'' (p. xv).

Fables appear in both the *Spectator* and the *Tatler,* and Joseph Addison enthusiastically treated them in articles and numerous comments. He emphasizes in one article the status of fables as ''the first pieces of wit'' that the world knew and remarks the esteem for them both ''in times of greatest simplicity'' and in ''the most polite ages of mankind. . . . As fables took their Birth in the very Infancy of Learning, they never flourished more than when Learning was at its greatest Height.'' [16] Addison's notion of the fable, however, seems to blend the broad definition of Boileau (whom he mentions) with the more precise Aesopian one of later commentators. He interprets it as a moral story but includes moral allegory or allegorical romance—Spenser's *Faerie Queene,* for example—and explains that while some fables personify ''Brutes and vegetables,'' others restrict themselves to human characters; and a third category employs ''Passions, Virtues, Vices.'' An example of his own creation personifies pleasure, virtue, happiness, and other abstract qualities.

In another *Spectator* essay Addison analyzes the purpose and method of the fable. Nobody hears advice without experiencing a surge of resentment: ''We look upon the Man who gives it us as offering an Affront to our Understanding, and treating us like Children or Idiots.'' [17] Since a posture of superiority inevitably accompanies advice, Addison warns that nothing is more difficult to accomplish without giving offense. Thus the invention of various instructional devices, among which the fable is supremely agreeable and effective. It creates the impression of self-guidance: one reads the fable to enjoy the entertaining narrative; the moral, insinuating itself unawares, seems an original thought. The sense of participation and the pride involved in the discovery of the moral delight the reader. Addison summarizes the fable as an ''oblique manner of giving advice,'' inoffensive, and even ingratiating.

Samuel Croxall's *Fables of Aesop* (1722) epitomizes, to an ex-

tent, the fable in England: instruction alternates with politics and occasional bursts of vituperation, although his tend to be devoid of the
satire and humor that characterize some of his fabulizing compatriots.
Croxall quotes Addison on the venerability and efficacy of the genre
and apologizes for offering the English public a new edition "of what
it has had so often, and in so many Forms already." [18] No edition
worth noting has appeared since L'Estrange's, on the other hand, and
Croxall cites L'Estrange on the poor quality of fables available in his
own time. Having terminated his introductory graces, Croxall launches
an attack on "the Insufficiency of *L'Estrange's* own Performance."
Children would end up morally emaciated, even diabolic, if fed on his
fables, which foster "his pernicious Principles! Principles, coin'd and
suited to promote the growth, and serve the ends of Popery and Arbi-
trary Power." Croxall broadly intimates that L'Estrange formulated
his fables expressly to undermine the moral and patriotic fiber of British youth and thereby subvert British church and state. A Church of
England clergyman, Croxall provides a clue to the method of
L'Estrange's Jacobite perfidy when he declares that L'Estrange, trans-
gressing Aesop's basic principle of liberty, "perverts both the Sense
and Meaning of several Fables; particularly when any political Instruction is couch'd in the Application." Croxall, of course, endeavors to
counteract L'Estrange's pernicious principles.

All evidence points to the conclusion that the fable enjoyed scant
literary status in the seventeenth century. Few people considered it
worth critical attention, even in later years of the century when, after
La Fontaine, volumes of fables appeared with increasing regularity.
Literary society snubbed it as a harmless, although, it was hoped, instructive, little tale for children. From all indications the fable first
rose to prominence beyond the children's world as popular rather than
cultivated literature. Political writers and social satirists took advantage of its popular appeal, especially in England; and the political-
social fable frequently prevailed. John Gay's fables, the acme of the
genre in England, demonstrate the prevailing social trend. Gay wrote
his first volume (1727) on request for the educational use of the young

Duke of Cumberland, and he strove for both morality and originality.[19] It is doubtful, however, if one could classify these fables as children's literature. Social morals preponderating, they concern such matters as reputation, gossip, and vanity. They tend toward satire rather than moral instruction, and an underlying cynicism frequently comes to the surface. In his second volume of fables (1738), Gay does not pretend to appeal to children. The advertisement describes them as "mostly on subjects of a graver and more political turn." [20] They deal with corrupt politicians, social parasites, and fools, including a fable titled "The Degenerate Bees," which seems a reply to Mandeville: virtue does exist in this society of bees, but it survives only in a harassed, even besieged, minority.

Gay's political and social concern places him in the mainstream of English fable writing. The social-political focus frequently results in fables considerably more interesting than the dutifully moral ones; but at the same time the concern with contemporary matters exposes them to classification as *Tendenzdichtung* or, at worst, hack writing. The association of the English fable with sixpenny pamphlets and hack writers substantially explains why it failed to attain the status of a respectable literary genre, which its French and German counterparts achieved. Even later in the century, when writers in the continental countries enthusiastically produced original fables and pondered theories of the genre, volumes published in England tended to contain the traditional Aesopian ones, directed toward children. If original, they offered lightly disguised political tracts or aimed for wit, even flippancy, to while away idle hours.

CHAPTER FOUR

Theories of the Fable: La Motte and Richer

Antoine Houdar de La Motte is one of those many literary figures who eke out measures of renown in their own lifetimes but end up forgotten by later generations. They merit footnotes or perhaps fleeting assessments in the more thorough literary histories; but aside from the historical specialist, no one reads their works anymore.

La Motte would not have achieved even that contemporary measure of success if he had succumbed to the dismal failure on the Paris stage of his first play, a comedy, in 1693. The humiliation nearly drove him into a Trappist monastery. Four years later he returned to the theater, however, and subsequently achieved considerable success as an author of tragedies, opera lyrics, and ballet themes. Later came his odes, fables, and a steady stream of graceful prose, a portion of it dedicated to a polite defense of the Moderns in the sporadic Ancients-Moderns dispute. In 1710 La Motte was rewarded for his accomplishments by election to the French Academy.

Such was the course of a comfortable, although sometimes controversial, literary career. However, whatever else he might have accomplished or attempted, it is La Motte as fabulist and especially as author of an essay on the fable who assumes a significant role in this discussion.

In 1719 La Motte published his *Fables nouvelles*. The essay "Discourse on the Fable," which introduces the collection, is notable as the first theoretical treatment of the Aesopian fable in its own right.

Even though most of La Motte's insights are adaptations of standard critical precepts of the time and thus are not wholly original, later commentators on the genre typically recognize La Motte's fundamental position in fable theory. The "Discourse," as well as La Motte's fables, will come up for mention or assessment time and again in the following chapters. Also noteworthy is La Motte's unqualified use of "fable" in its narrower sense, referring to the Aesopian variety, which indicates that the broad meaning of plot or narrative was receding in currency by this time.

La Motte begins the "Discourse" with a eulogy of both Aesop and La Fontaine, but he seizes the opportunity for a brief foray into the Ancients-Moderns controversy. He refuses to compare the two fabulists, asserting the distinctive beauties and graces of both classic and modern; but he points out the antiquity of veneration of the Ancients in itself: the Romans revered Greek art and culture. The Ancients deserve the admiration accorded them; but La Motte complains that study of the masters frequently deteriorates into memorization and copying, a tendency which he condemns, declaring that any esthetic form or style represents just one of many possible ways of expression. Having declared his impartiality, the comments on the Ancients-Moderns relationship provide the opening for critical thrusts at La Fontaine. La Motte makes no claim to equality with his predecessor in the field of poetic beauty but boasts the originality of his own fables, in contrast to those of La Fontaine who merely borrowed and reworked the traditional ones.

La Motte defines the fable as "an instruction disguised under the allegory of an action," [1] which echoes Le Bossu's definition of "fable" in the inclusive sense of plot or narrative. Continuing in the apparent footsteps of Le Bossu, La Motte discerns close ties between the fable and the epic: the former is "a small epic poem, which yields nothing to the grander one but extensiveness, and which less constrained in the choice of characters can choose as it likes from nature that which it pleases to have act and speak for its purpose" (p. xi). La Motte apparently draws the comparison from Le Bossu, but his ver-

sion oversimplifies and even distorts his mentor's reference to Aesopian fable and epic *fable*. More than just length separates the two
genres. La Motte's comparison provides excellent advertisement for
the lesser genre, however, especially in its vaunted advantage over
epic—greater freedom in choice of characters.

La Motte traces the success of the fable to its indirectness and to
the involvement of the reader which pursuit of a hidden moral invites.
Both of these advantages Addison, for one, had observed earlier. No
one welcomes direct, didactic precepts, which inevitably arouse resistance and resentment, just as commands do. The fable functions
obliquely, allowing the reader himself to search for the truth; and the
sense of personal discovery impels him to believe it. La Motte portrays the life of Aesop, a slave, according to tradition, as a fable in itself. A slave must approach truths warily and express them subtly,
since his master expects him to entertain, not preach. This master-
slave relationship, claims La Motte, metaphorically describes the situation of all fabulists.

Although entertaining, the fable must, nevertheless, instruct:
"But it would be something monstrous to imagine a Fable without instructive aim. Its essence is to be a symbol and consequently to signify
something else than what it says literally. . . . The Fable is a disguised
Philosophy, which does not banter except to instruct, and which
always instructs more than it amuses" (p. xiii). The fable insinuates
its lesson by way of the senses, which La Motte declares the most effective method of instruction. The instruction itself should normally
consist of a moral truth: "It develops in us that germ of right and of
justice which nature put there, and which only too often is choked out
by our passions" (p. xiv). A moral truth is preferable, but the fabulist
should in any case avoid trivialities and stupidities.

The imagery of the fable should be unified, suitable, and natural,
or, if not based on nature, it should at least have a foundation in popular opinion. La Motte criticizes Aesop for occasional lapses from nature: for example, the fable in which a lion falls in love with a girl and
seeks to marry her. He claims that the notion of a lion courting a

maiden clashes with the reader's sense of natural order, resulting in the ultimate ridiculousness of the entire fable. Animals, nevertheless, are the most eminently appropriate personages, to the extent that they are often considered essential; but La Motte asserts that other actors can also be cast, such as men and plants, although he doubts the efficacy of machines. The style of the fable, he continues, should be familiar rather than elevated; but familiarity does not exclude elegance. The familiar style enhances the necessary humor, which derives from the endowment of animals with human qualities or, stated more broadly, from the bestowal of great qualities on lesser things.

La Motte's own fables suffer from excessive length because of protracted introductory comments on human nature, politics, and writing—even advice on how to compose fables. Often the prologue equals the fable in length. La Motte, more a man of ideas than a poet, defended the superiority of prose over poetry; [2] and most of his best writing is in prose. For some reason he constructed his own fables in verse, perhaps because he preferred Phaedrus to Aesop or because he felt compelled to challenge La Fontaine. His verse, in any case, tends to be ponderous and prosaic.

La Motte was both influential and controversial during his own lifetime and throughout the eighteenth century. He wrote in all genres and constructed theories of them all. Nor did he shrink from changing his mind. In the Ancients-Moderns controversy, for example, he apparently shifted sides more than once. He attracted both praise and ridicule. His odes seemed to elicit preponderant acclaim in his own lifetime, while his fables provoked harsh criticism and parodies—even a play mocking him as a fabulist. [3] Later in the century, however, his renown shifted to his fables, where it remained as long as fables continued in vogue. When the genre drifted into obscurity, La Motte accompanied it.

Despite the ambiguities of his reputation, La Motte inspired much of the fable writing and theorizing, especially the latter, that resulted in acceptance of the fable as a literary genre. Sometimes denigrated as a fabulist, although more frequently ranked second to La Fontaine

among the Moderns, he invariably received credit as the father of fable
theory—a considerable honor in a century that took theory seriously.
When later critics and fabulists discuss the conceptual roots of the
genre, they normally begin with La Motte and proceed from his
ground-breaking discourse. In the 1730's and 1740's, therefore, as interest in the fable increases momentously, we shall see that the fable
writer normally turns to Aesop, Phaedrus, and La Fontaine for guidance; but the critic first consults La Motte.

Henri Richer, a minor literary figure whose *Fables nouvelles* appeared in 1729, represents an exception, however, for he does not
mention his predecessor La Motte. The omission is all the more surprising since Richer's lengthy preface amounts to an essay on the fable
and would seem to call for remarks on the earlier one, only ten years
before, even if to disagree.

Richer recognizes that some poetic genres, such as the pastoral,
have no purpose but "honest amusement"; [4] but he maintains that
those which endeavor to correct morals achieve a higher excellence.
The fable epitomizes the second category: it both pleases and instructs—and perhaps carries out its aim more effectively than any
other kind of poetry. Human nature forbids scrutiny of unshaded
truths, the glare of which disturbs the ego. Confronted with abstract
precepts, moreover, or even esteemed personages as examples to follow, most people fabricate excuses and unblushingly shrug off their
weaknesses; but they will find no excuse for ignoring a lesson they see
acted out "by Bees and Ants: they will be ashamed to be subjected to
the passions of the most despicable animals" (p. xi). The argument
resembles Furetière's: utilization of animals ensures disinterested
teaching, thereby eliminating the resentment that instruction by a fellow man arouses. At the same time, observing dumb animals behave
themselves better than we do evokes a sense of shame. The result is a
truth made palpable, driven home without the reader being aware of its
presence.

If this educational process seems too smooth and effortless,
arousing scepticism about such uncomplicated human enlightenment,

Richer shares the skepticism. He does not delude himself as to the desires of most people: "It is true that few people regard poetry as instructive. One goes to a comedy to laugh and to look to see if one cannot find in it the likeness of his neighbor. One seeks in a satire the pleasure of seeing others made ridiculous" (p. xii). Fables represent no exception. People peruse them for amusement and rarely take cognizance of the underlying moral lesson. The least perceptive go no farther than the external image and the simple narrative. Most others grasp the allegory but pervert the applications. Few people profit from the moral. Moral instruction is exceedingly difficult even under ideal conditions. In order to circumvent the difficulties as far as possible, Richer stresses that the fable must concomitantly entertain, as must all literature that aims to instruct. People will assiduously study a work of history or philosophy written in the most atrocious style; but they immediately abandon a bad poem, regardless of the message it contains. Poetic success, moreover, is particularly elusive with the fable, which has been taken to its highest point of perfection. That high point of perfection refers, of course, to the accomplishment of La Fontaine. All subsequent fabulists must sail in his wake, under constant danger of being swamped by unfavorable comparison with him. If the aspiring fabulist succumbs to this impossible comparison, the likelihood of inculcating a lesson, slim at best, becomes nil.

According to Richer's definition, "the fable is a fiction, which contains a precept hidden under an allegorical image" (p. xiii). Success prescribes that the image be appropriate (*juste*) and natural. Naturalness prevails if the image remains probable and if "nothing is contrary to the instinct of the animals, usual characters of the Apologue." To be appropriate, it must "present simply and without mistake the action and the characters" (p. xiv). Richer affirms that even the Ancients did not always adhere to these rules, for example, in the narrative already criticized by La Motte of a lion falling in love with a girl, or in the equally unnatural situation of a sophist wolf bothering to pick a quarrel with a forlorn lamb in order to justify devouring him. Referring specifically to the latter example, Richer locates the fundamental difficulty in the conflict between conformity to nature and the necessity of portraying anthropomorphized beasts. He declares that few fables manage strict adherence to the rules and that the onerousness of doing so calls for critical indulgence.

The animal world, nevertheless, supplies the usual and most effective personages: the majority resemble us; their actions being a "naive depiction of ours," they lack only the power of speech. Personages can also be fabricated from plants and material objects—all according to the discretion of the fabulist—but Richer discourages the use of mythological figures and excludes abstract qualities: "The allegories should be chosen from physical objects which strike the senses. The aim of the apologue is to make moral maxims palpable: it is therefore not necessary to hide these abstract truths under a metaphysical veil. To do so would be to show little knowledge of the spirit of poetry, which loves palpable images, and in particular would transgress the rules of the fable, which should be at the reach of the less intelligent" (pp. xvi–xvii). Familiar characters ensure interest in and understanding of the narrative, resulting in easier discovery of the hidden truth, especially for children and the average man.

Stylistically, the fabulist should aim for simplicity and a kind of "elegant naiveté," qualities which bestow a traditional charm on the fable and which surpass regularity in importance. Both "simplicity" and "naiveté" become bywords of later commentators on the fable. In all aspects of style Richer extols the supremacy of La Fontaine, who, profitably imitating the Ancients, joined Aesop's simplicity and naiveté to Phaedrus's grace and elegance. Richer prescribes adherence to one's own genius but carefully limits originality to subject matter and imagery. In other aspects of fable composition, such as "expression," emulation of Phaedrus and La Fontaine is equivalent to following nature. Richer possibly intends his advice about the limits of originality to be an oblique criticism of La Motte and his boasts of innovation.

Finally, Richer prescribes no set length for a fable but remarks that in general brevity expedites memorization and thereby enhances

moral utility, especially for young people. The moral lesson, furthermore, should normally form the conclusion, where the sense of discovery augments its effectiveness.

His own volume, Richer explains, comprises both original and
borrowed fables, the latter having been furnished with at least "a new
image" (p. xxv). The moral lessons themselves cannot be too
frequently repeated. As to possible accusations that his fables compare
unfavorably with La Fontaine's, Richer claims that a poet can be
honorably second-rate: rejection of works lacking excellence would
destroy the viability of existing genres, since each contains creations
of standard-setting sublimity. One must take into account, moreover,
that individual works possess distinctive beauties and merits.

La Motte and Richer seem to be in essential agreement about the
fable. Both describe an allegorical form with an entertaining fiction or
action disguising an edifying lesson. Both men, products of their age,
expect an element of didacticism in all literature and therefore welcome a genre that offers an easy, straightforward combination of literature and lesson. Both trace the fable's pedagogical effectiveness to
the indirect approach and the transformation of abstract principles into
readily graspable illustrations. Both prescribe a simple or familiar
style, yet with a touch of elegance. Both, again products of their age,
respect rules and tradition, even though La Motte stresses the innovative nature of his fables and Richer emphasizes the limits of innovation
and the value of studying the historical model. Both, finally, give
serious attention to a literary form which normally had not received it.

Despite the agreements, Richer's discussion emerges as the most
perceptive and judicious. He carefully analyzes the fable and recommends its blend of diversion and didacticism, but he also warns that
instruction is always a serious and difficult business. In other words,
he expects no miracles from his or any other fables or any teaching
device. La Motte, on the other hand, apparently intended his "Discourse" to be primarily an introduction to and advertisement for his
volume of fables. His rather sensationalistic comparison of fable and

epic, for example, rings like the blurb on a modern paperback. His critical observations are normally valid, but no one could accuse him of excessive profundity.

It is difficult to believe that Richer was not acquainted with La Motte's work by the time of his own fables and the accompanying preface. The more likely alternative suggests that, although familiar with it, he chose to ignore it except in such innuendos as his remarks on originality. Richer's conspicuous humility contrasts with La Motte's boasts of originality and none-too-subtle disparagement of La Fontaine. Whatever the merits of the two critical treatises, however, Richer's remained in relative obscurity while La Motte's attracted attention and exercised influence, probably due to La Motte's greater personal and literary prestige and to the earlier date of publication. Later fabulists and critics customarily acknowledge La Motte, whereas few seem aware of Richer's existence.

eclectic borrowings for his *Versuch in poetischen Fabeln und Er-zählungen* (*Experiment in Poetical Fables and Stories,* 1729) emerges substantial originality. In introducing the volume, Hagedorn bows respectfully before his master La Fontaine but defends his artistic dignity by pointing out that La Fontaine himself had Phaedrus for a model. In this way, Hagedorn suggests his own position at the continuing end of a venerable line of tradition. But having reached well beyond the French master for inspiration, he acknowledges in footnotes and in the table of contents his diverse sources, which include various Latin fabulists, La Motte, Gay, L'Estrange, Prior, Swift, and other English poets. Denying that he has merely translated, however, Hagedorn explains his "Experiment" as "a free imitation of Ancients and Moderns" that provides ample range for poetic originality.[1] The title also indicates his experimentation with various poetical forms and styles in an attempt to arrive at a creation typically his own and, in a broader sense, to contribute to the formation of a native German literature.

The latter element also accounts for the qualification *"Versuch"* in Johann Christoph Gottsched's *Versuch einer critischen Dichtkunst für die Deutschen* (*Attempt at a Critical Poetics for Germans,* 1730). Faced with the virtual absence of a functioning German literary tradition, Gottsched undertakes in this work to lay the foundation for one with material mined largely from French classicism, causing later German writers and critics to object that his plans called for nothing more than reconstruction of French literary culture on German soil. In view of his admiring dependence on traditional authorities such as Boileau, it is not surprising that Gottsched interprets fable as essentially plot or narrative. To compose one, he prescribes as the first step selection of "an instructive moral thesis," which will form the foundation of the entire poetical work.[2] The second step calls for an event which promises vivid illustration of the selected lesson; and only the third and final step, utilization of the event or creation of the fable, manifests generic distinctions. Gottsched, like Boileau and other classicists, regards characterization as the fundamental distinction between genres. The epic, tragic, comic, and Aesopian fables seem to comprise the principal kinds, although Gottsched treats others, such as the "sybaritic fable," the joking, lightly satiric story. This latter category incurs his disparagement, however: "Poetry was invented for nobler purposes than simply to make men more pompous and debauched" (p. 445). And he regrets that many of La Fontaine's fables belong to the sybaritic category.

In the construction of an Aesopian fable Gottsched specifies that the initial step, the same as for any other kind, is to select an instructive moral thesis. Characteristically, however, the Aesopian fable endeavors to instruct the common man, to teach him moral truths under pleasant images, which serve to "sweeten the bitter lessons" (p. 446). Gottsched thus associates the Aesopian fable with the common man, although he underscores its instructive value for young people of all social levels. Once the moral lesson has been selected, the next stop is to incorporate it into a suitable action that concerns plants, trees, or animals. Gottsched stresses that the situation and circumstances of the fable must conform to nature. A predatory animal, for example, must behave godlessly and unjustly; a brightly colored tulip appropriately symbolizes vanity. But the fabulist may avail himself of any segment of creation with only the slightest appearance of morality. Nor does Gottsched exclude human beings as potential characters; when they appear, the fable appertains to the sub-category *Erzählung* or *conte* (short story). Thus, according to Gottsched's system the short story, or its ancestor, which would develop into a major literary genre in the nineteenth century, exists as a sub-category of the Aesopian fable.

Gottsched urges brevity, warning that unnecessary prolongation of the narrative disserves the moral purpose. He complains, moreover, that Aesop's exemplary simplicity and brevity have evaded successful imitation by modern fabulists: "All the newer fabulists, from La Fontaine on, up to the most recent, are, on the contrary, often great chatterers" (pp. 448–49). They prolong the narrative by inserting superfluous details and diversions that cause the average reader to overlook the main, moral point; and many modern fabulists concentrate on cleverness or humor, giving only fleeting attention to the moral purpose.

Gottsched singles out La Motte, among others, to illustrate these failings. He maintains, however, that brevity and simplicity do not preclude stylistic refinement; and again the classical masters Aesop and Phaedrus serve him as examples.

Gottsched's discussion of the fable in the general sense of plot or narrative follows strict classical lines, which is not surprising considering his affinity for classical rules and order. His treatment of the Aesopian fable depicts a no-nonsense didactic tool. It aims to teach a moral lesson; and Gottsched allows no fripperies, nothing that does not contribute directly to the moral aim. His discussion also emanates a note of condescension: the Aesopian fable is fine for children and the common man, but the intelligent adult should be able to swallow the bitter moral pill without the sugar-coating of a superimposed fiction. To a lesser extent the same might be said of all literature, since Gottsched demands a conscious moral lesson at the core of any literary work.

On the other hand, the mere presence of the discussion of the Aesopian fable in *Versuch einer critischen Dichtkunst* reveals the prestige acquired by the literary form since the days of Boileau, who did not deign to discuss it. Gottsched, writing some half-century later, apparently considers it one of the four principal literary genres, although the least of the four.

In later years Gottsched had to suffer accusations of anachronism and obsequious imitation for proposing the installation of seventeenth-century French classicism in eighteenth-century Germany. His conservative ideas and traditional models clashed with the assertive self-awareness and progressive urge of young German literary talent. The resulting antagonism erupted in the literary war between Gottsched and his followers on the one side and the Swiss Johann Jakob Bodmer and Johann Jacob Breitinger and their followers on the other. The majority of the Swiss faction rejected Gottsched's French literary models as obsolete or reactionary and turned to English ones, which they considered to be paving the way of the future. Gottsched, to illustrate further the field of contention, labored to build a functioning German theater, virtually non-existent at that time. With his six-volume *Deutsche Schaubühne* (*German Stage*), he offered a repertory and, for budding German playwrights, a wealth of examples, all classically oriented, of course, and most, translations of French dramas. Bodmer, Breitinger, and others of their persuasion preferred the freer, unities-ignoring style of Shakespeare and other English dramatists. And so the lines were drawn and the battles fought. The war ended with Gottsched's utter defeat, to the point that even in his lifetime his name frequently was used as a synonym for pedantic foolishness.

During the years it was fought, the literary battle shifted between several fronts. Along with representatives of other genres, fabulists and fable critics from both ideological camps became entangled in the controversy. At times they occupied the turbulent center of attention.

Daniel Wilhelm Triller and Daniel Stoppe were fabulists who supported Gottsched. The former published his *Neue äsopische Fabeln* (*New Aesopian Fables*) in 1737, the latter, his *Neue Fabeln oder moralische Gedichte* (*New Fables or Moral Poems*) in the following year. Triller's volume bears the subtitle "wherein diverse edifying moral lessons and useful rules of conduct are expounded in metrical speech," which to the twentieth-century reader conveys a humorous ring of smug sermonizing. Eighteenth-century Germans apparently accepted the advertisement in all sincerity, a difference in outlook which helps to explain the popularity of fables and other didactic literature in that period. Both Triller and Stoppe were forced to endure or repel repeated critical assaults on their fables by acid-penned warriors of the Swiss faction. Triller, in addition, composed an extensive essay on the genre, which was also subjected to heavy critical attack.

Triller commences his essay, which first appeared as a preface to his fables, by emphasizing the venerability of the genre. He laments, however, that the modern world—and particularly the German part—has tended to ignore it, producing few noteworthy fables. This deficiency parallels a woeful lack of German accomplishment in the epic, leading Triller to speculate that perhaps aspiring poets eschew the one because of its intimidating length and arduousness and the other because it appears ridiculously short and easy. The dual purpose of his own work, he declares, is to dispell this condescending estimation and to alleviate the scarcity of German fables.

Triller initially praises La Motte's "Discourse" to the point of labeling it definitive, but then promptly qualifies this estimate by declaring that he does have a few critical remarks of his own to interpose. One of them concerns the relationship of fable and epic. Triller, as noted above, deplores the paucity of German accomplishment in both genres; but in regard to the genres themselves, he perceives no similarities and, therefore, challenges La Motte's definition of the fable as "a small epic poem." There are vast differences, he claims, between the two literary modes. The fable, on the one hand, is "short, simple, lively, comical, natural, and at the end witty." [3] The epic, on the other hand, is "long, serious, artificially developed, exalted, and, so to speak, supernatural" (p. 594). Triller apparently has no knowledge of the relationship between the two as originally postulated by Le Bossu, to which he would perhaps subscribe; but his rejection of La Motte's misrepresentation seems justified, if also somewhat simplistic in manner of performance.

Triller vigorously asserts that the moral tag should terminate the fable: beginning with it is comparable to serving the dessert before the soup (p. 595). La Motte proposes the same order, but Triller accuses him of inconsistency in actual practice. La Motte, moreover, often prefaces his fables with long, rambling introductions, which Triller applauds as "very pretty, witty, noble and edifying," but he opines that the reader would enjoy them more if encountered elsewhere: the entrance to La Motte's house typically overwhelms, in both extent and extravagance, the house itself (p. 597). Triller hastily denies any intended criticism of the French fabulist: he is merely attempting to warn subsequent practitioners of the genre not to follow his misguided path.

Every fable, continues Triller, must include "something *unbelievable* but at the same time nothing *irrational* or *unnatural*" (p. 598). He insists that this "unbelievable" element constitutes the essence of the fable; without it the fable degenerates into an ordinary story. He stresses, however—as do Gottsched and most commentators on the genre—that the "unbelievable" must not contradict reason or nature, in which case the moral would lose relevance and the fable would deteriorate into a joke. A fox conversing with a rooster or a wolf with a lamb, for example, is quite acceptable; both situations are *unbelievable,* but neither one is *unnatural.* Although incapable of verbal expression, animals do emit sounds and possess the fundamental tools of speech. Only a "conceited Cartesian," therefore, would deny them all ability to communicate and refuse them a certain concomitant reasoning capacity (p. 600). A fox flying to the limb of an oak tree to chat with a raven, on the other hand, or a wolf transporting her young to a stork's nest high on a church tower exceeds all possibility. Since neither animal possesses physical attributes that even remotely suggest the ability to fly, an airborne fox or wolf is not only unbelievable but also irrational and unnatural. The fable of the fox and the grapes meets acceptable standards of credibility, but the one relating the encounter of the fox with the statue does not. Why would a fox enter a sculptor's workshop, and how could he pass judgment on man's power of reason? The Biblical fable of the briar that desires to marry the cedar is acceptable, since both parties involved are plants; but Richer's creation recounting the matrimonial longings of a butterfly for a flower is not. Triller also concurs in La Motte's strictures on the lack of verisimilitude in La Fontaine's fable, derived from Aesop, in which a lion proposes marriage to a girl.

While undue exaggeration of the unbelievable element results in ridiculousness, Triller warns that a fable also risks failure at the contrary extreme of excessive naturalness and rationality. For example, a fox steals a chicken from a farmer; the farmer kills the fox. Moral: failure to respect the possessions of others can lead to fatal consequences. The narrative relates a common daily event worth scant notice; it offers nothing unbelievable and, therefore, lacks the essential quality of a fable. Human characters intensify the danger of excessive naturalness, an observation which causes Triller to admonish that a narrative relying exclusively on human beings is, strictly speaking, "not a true and complete fable" (p. 608).

Triller's choice of terminology for his discussion seems rather unfortunate. He employs "unbelievable" (*unglaublich*) for the most important characteristic of the fable, whereas "irrational" (*unvernünftig*) denotes ridiculousness and failure. The two terms represent, however, degrees of an identical quality and fail to mark lucidly the intended difference. "Wonder," adopted subsequently by the critic Johann Jacob Breitinger, describes the quality more accurately than Triller's "unbelievable." Triller's concern with naturalness, nevertheless, signalizes a problem that invariably troubles theoreticians and critics of the fable. His is far from the last word we shall hear on the question of how far poetic license can extend the mental capabilities of a fox or the marital possibilities of a lion.

In the second, expanded edition of his fables (1740) Triller replaced the original preface with a more succinct one that omits mention of the unbelievable. This shorter essay lists in parallel dichotomies two kinds of fables: "narrating and narrated," "dialogic and historical," or "conversation and story" fables.[4] The first of each dichotomy grants the power of speech to normally mute personages, whereas the second simply narrates their activities. Triller prefers the first method. He also emphasizes the necessity for an intelligible, useful moral and accuses La Motte of speaking over the heads of his audience. Stylistically the fable should be natural, he maintains, but not vulgar; it should also be brief and direct, avoiding ornamentation and digressions. Triller devotes the remainder of this introduction to proving the worth of fables, for which purpose he cites an array of authorities from ancient times to modern.

Triller, as previously noted, attended Gottsched's literary school; both his fables and treatises drew derisive criticism from the opposing forces of Bodmer and Breitinger. He apparently withdrew the original introductory essay to his fables because of critical attacks on it. Foremost among his attackers stood Johann Jacob Breitinger himself, who devoted half of the one hundred-page chapter on the fable in his *Critische Dichtkunst* (*Critical Poetics*, 1740) to critically mauling Triller.

Basic to Breitinger's entire poetics is his concept of wonder—*das Wunderbare*—in literature, an idea which he had developed previously in dealing with Milton's *Paradise Lost*. He discerned in the fable a superior example of how wonder underlies literary creation, which partially accounts for the extended treatment of the genre in his *Critische Dichtkunst*. Aesop, he explains, initially drew his stories from observations of daily life; but common daily experiences in themselves contain nothing to arouse interest. The fabulist recognized the deficiency and turned to the animal world in order to inject an element of strangeness, or precisely Breitinger's wonder. Wonder, declares Breitinger, can be aroused by two fundamental methods: by giving an unexpected turn of events to the plot or by adopting animals, plants, gods, or other unreal or normally lifeless creatures and objects as characters. Aesop chose the latter, which has remained the characteristic method of the fabulist.

Breitinger defines the fable in terms that accentuate the role of wonder: "The fable, its essence and origin considered, is nothing other than an instructive wonder." [5] Although its nature is exotic, its purpose is ineluctably practical; and Breitinger's explanation parallels what we have heard before: the fable was invented in order morally to instruct and to remind in a disguised and agreeable manner. It clothes "dry and bitter" truths in a charming mask in order to ensure their unresisted acceptance into the human heart. People usually construe direct moral truths and lessons to be complaints or punishment and consequently resist them. The combination of story-telling and wonder, however, attracts attention, maintains interest, and discretely inculcates the moral lesson without provoking resentment. Breitinger insists that the fabulist, avoiding all appearance of teacher or judge, must entertain; and he compares the fable to a diverting comedy in which animals serve as actors. The reader should remain unaware of the intended moral instruction until the end, where, captivated by the charm of the fable, he will good-humoredly benefit from it.

Breitinger divides literary wonder into three categories, based on degrees of reality, but emphasizes that the bounds of possibility should never be exceeded (pp. 186 ff.). The first category, employing ordinary mortals, effectuates a fable more plausible than wondrous. The second one exploits other living beings and inanimate things, while the third presents a combination of the other two. The categories are variations of the traditional classical ones; but whereas Le Bossu and others utilize them to denote fable in the inclusive sense of plot or narrative, Breitinger applies them exclusively to the Aesopian fable. He vigorously, and rather curiously, denies that human characters inhibit creation of a true, "wonder-arousing" fable, now implying that wonder and poetry are no more than agreeable side effects and that a genuine fable can be constructed without them. The point is confusing. Breitinger's sudden spirited defense of human actors and "realistic" fables seems to contradict his own essential concept of literary wonder. Presumably he undertakes it to confound Triller, who doubted the feasibility of a genuine fable using exclusively human characters. Direct references to Triller emerge later in Breitinger's discussion.

Breitinger, such puzzling disclaimers aside, devotes considerable space to justification of the wondrous element. Denying that talking, reasoning animals provoke any deep-seated incredulity, he remarks upon the close relationship of animals to human beings and cites the instance of people who work with mute beasts and frequently acquire the habit of talking to them. Nor does he find any valid reason to doubt the capability of animals to converse among themselves; fables simply translate their idiom into language intelligible to men. Nor do gods and mythological figures elude credibility, since all people recognize and accept them. Plants and other inanimate things, however, bear with them the danger of exceeding the limits of possibility and of thus arriving at ridiculousness. Breitinger warns that a fabulist availing himself of such characters must exercise extreme care. If, on the other hand, the fabulist must choose between adhering to the observations of natural science or following traditional opinion, however misguided it might be, he should select the latter course.

Breitinger extols La Motte's fables and critical principles and borrows his concepts, for example, a definition—one of several formulated at various points in his discussion—that could pass for a translation from the French: the fable is "a reminder which is hidden under the allegory of an action" (p. 168). Breitinger also praises the diversional "Episodia" which grace the beginnings of La Motte's fables, those long introductions caustically described by Triller as the entrances to La Motte's houses larger and more lavish than the houses themselves. At another point, however, Breitinger declares the necessity for unity and precision. He also subscribes to the intimate relationship of fable and epic postulated by La Motte: the fable is "a small and compact epic poem. Both belong to the same genus and have the same essence. . . . In both the action which is narrated must be only simple and have a primary lesson for its purpose" (p. 195). Apparently having read further than his French mentor, however, Breitinger refers to the Aesopian fable and the epic fable, not to the epic as such. He equates the form of the two but differentiates their length, characters, and ideals.

Breitinger also calls upon the familiar analogy of body and soul, the former comprising the narrative of the fable, the latter the moral lesson. He insists that the body exists solely as a container for the soul and limits the former to circumstances pertinent to the ultimate moral point. At this juncture he allows no *episodia*. The exclusiveness of the moral concern, moreover, distinguishes the fable from the history and the story, both of which illustrate a moral truth only incidentally. The fable, furthermore, requires an *allegorical* narrative, without which it degenerates into "empty child's play" (p. 172). But through the allegorical screen the underlying moral lesson should be easily discernible without resorting to deep thought, obviating the need for an attached moral to elucidate it. Aesop constructed his fables in this way and never appended moral tags. Breitinger retreats from this ideal immediately after stating it, however, and admits that the varied tastes and capabilities of readers often make an attached moral advisable; but it should always conclude the fable. Otherwise it destroys the entertaining mask, the most formidable pedagogical asset of the fable, by announcing at the outset the instructive intention. Breitinger points to Phaedrus as a cautionary example: the Latin fabulist frequently proclaims his intended moral at the beginning and consequently must depend on admiration for his art to maintain the reader's attention.

The thoroughness and intensity of Breitinger's protracted assault on Triller's fables and concepts indicates that his aim was annihilation rather than constructive criticism. He condemns Triller for failure consistently to place the moral at the end, where they both agree it should be. He accuses him of flagrant deviations from nature, i.e., of exceeding possibility and concocting sheer fantasy. He ridicules Triller's choice of moral lessons, labeling them strange or irrelevant. He censures him for portraying animals that behave like four-legged human beings, devoid of bestial attributes other than their names. Discarding his rival's poetic pretensions with a single, sweeping comment, Breitinger accuses Triller of totally lacking artistic sense and taste. Most puzzling, however, is Breitinger's condemnation of the unbelievable concept, a quality which, it will be recalled, Triller declared essential to the fable. Breitinger himself interchanges Triller's term with his own "wonder," and the two critics seem to designate an identical property with their respective terms. Breitinger, moreover, stresses the importance of wonder as much, if not more, than Triller—for example, when he defines the fable as "an instructive wonder." In the course of his unrelenting assault on Triller, nevertheless, he reverses himself, refuting the notion that a fable must contain unbelievability and even declaring fables with human characters to be superior (p. 234). At this point of his discussion Breitinger seems to say that the fable abandons stark realism reluctantly, only as a last resort; the ideal fable, rather than "an instructive wonder," would present an instructive commonplace.

Triller's fables, while not masterpieces, drew a considerable contemporary audience; and although his ideas fall short of brilliance, they flow smoothly with the mainstream of contemporary critical thought. Breitinger, it would seem, exhibits his own limitations in the process of exaggerating Triller's. In attempting to pulverize the latter's theoretical examination of the fable, moreover, he eulogizes La Motte's "Discourse" to such an extreme that it seems to represent his gospel of fable theory and practice. In the last line of the chapter Breitinger truculently advises Triller to consult La Motte.

Triller, declining to sit back and turn the other cheek to Breitinger's vituperations, defended himself in the 1740 second edition of his fables; and his defense was apparently stronger, if also cruder, in an earlier preface to this edition which was suppressed by the censor.[6] A copy of the earlier version fell into Breitinger's hands, however; and he printed it accompanied by an "Essential Supplementary Piece," which renewed his own attack. A certain Theodor Pitschel fought the next round for Triller in "Remarks on the Supplementary Piece," which appeared in three instalments in the periodical *Belustigungen des Verstandes und des Witzes* in August, September, and October 1741. Pitschel undertook his attack to defend Triller but subsequently expanded it to support Gottsched and the entire faction. Breitinger counterattacked, Bodmer joined in, and Triller himself returned their fire with another article of his own. His volley was apparently the last; the forces disengaged, and the war shifted to new territory, probably because neither faction could find fresh insults to sling at the other on this battlefield. Although nominally fought in the name of fables, the later skirmishes amounted to no more than personal attacks.

In 1748 an unsigned article "On the Fable" appeared in the moral weekly *Der Gesellige* which carries the concept of wonder to a logical extreme: the ideal fable becomes a fairy tale with a moral.

The author introduces his article by remarking the current popularity of the fable and expressing his assurance that *Gesellige* readers will, therefore, be interested in learning about its theoretical basis. He offers traditional explanations for the invention of it: everybody avoids recognition of his own faults; and the fable, like sugar, coats "the bitter pills of truth." [7] The principal device of the genre, use of animal characters, derives from an ancient belief that animals have a language which they use among themselves. Animal personages thus distinguish the true fable, which maintains only "poetic plausibility." The other kind of fable, the story (*Erzählung*), limits itself to human characters, thereby gaining realism but losing wonder. Consequently it ends up on the outer fringe of the genre, in the shadow of history.

Of the three fundamental qualities of the fable, plausibility urges assiduous imitation of nature: a cat must be false, a fox, clever, and so on. Inanimate things, the author warns, require particular vigilance in this regard. Plausibility connects the fable to reality; but its second quality, wonder, exerts pressure in the opposite direction. It serves to arouse the reader's curiosity, retain his attention, and concurrently make "a creator out of the poet" (p. 743). Wonder contrives, moreover, to attract adults as well as children: "It makes serious men just as attentive as children. The more higher powers, such as deities, angels, spirits, other fairies and sorcerers that are skillfully introduced, that much better is the fable, which will be scorned under the name of childish fairy tale only by the narrow-minded" (pp. 743–44). The author claims that the finest book of fables ever printed brings in a goblin, and he repeats his adversion to narrow-minded people who malign the genre as childish tales.

The fable does degenerate into a fairy tale, however, if it lacks the moral lesson, which constitutes its third quality and its very soul. The moral lesson should emerge conspicuously and naturally from the narrative and thus dispose of the need for an appended tag: "the reader is not so brainless that he cannot find the lesson" (p. 744). If the fabulist decides to explicate the moral, he at least should beware of insulting the reader's intelligence. Other qualities, such as humor and flowing style, enter into the composition of a fable; but the moral lesson, wonder, and a foundation in naturalness constitute the primary ones. The author, moreover, only grudgingly recognizes the realistic fable with human characters and even then relegates it to the shadowy borders of the genre. "An instructive wonder" would describe his notion of the fable even better than Breitinger's.

Johann Jakob Bodmer, who shared leadership of the rebellious Swiss literary faction with Breitinger, provided a "Critical Introduction" to Ludwig Meyer von Knonau's *Ein halbes Hundert neuer Fabeln* (*A Half-hundred New Fables,* 1744). The introduction adds nothing brilliant to fable theory, but it marks the beginning of Bodmer's interest in the subject. In the ensuing years, as we shall see, he applied himself to the fable on various occasions and even produced examples of his own.

In the "Critical Introduction" Bodmer, the inveterate enemy of classical imitation, stresses originality and proudly refers the reader to Meyer von Knonau's fables as a paragon of inventiveness: "These fables are not made by others and only redecorated; they belong to the author not only because of a few additions or because of the moral usage that he made of them. . . . He is more rightly their *creator,* in that he gave them not only their form but their being." [8] Bodmer designates two methods of conceiving a fable: the fabulist may begin with a moral lesson in mind and subsequently search for an appropriate illustration, or he may observe the behavior of animals and extract a moral lesson from his observations. Aesop employed the first method, which is superior; invention of an illustrative narrative requires greater talent and profounder knowledge of animals. The second approach, extracting a moral from an observed action, demands less knowledge but more hard work and luck: "the truth to tell, Fables of this second kind are not so much *invented* as *discovered.*" This method frequently serves the "fable catcher," the lighthearted dilettante who embarks on a "fable hunt" simply in order to produce a collection and who gives scant concern to the lessons they inculate. Bodmer admits that the reader remains unaffected by, and even unaware of, the creative method used, providing the plot is in accord with the moral lesson, like body and soul. He applauds Meyer von Knonau, as one might expect, for employing the preferred method, working from a preconceived moral lesson. How he knows this, Bodmer does not say.

Bodmer issues the customary edict about following nature, affirming that animal personages must behave in a manner reflecting their true characters, not in ways foreign to them or like "masked humans." If the fabulist deviates from natural traits, the fable tends to degenerate into a farce, which, of course, obliterates the moral lesson. Brevity is also important, especially when dealing with animals. Bodmer probes deeper into the shortcomings of animal characters in his subsequent *Kritische Briefe;* here he simply advises fabulists to include no more than the pertinent actions and immediate feelings of the actors, plus a short conclusion. Loquaciousness detracts from the dramatic effect. In this regard Bodmer accuses La Fontaine of enriching his creations with incidental decorations in order to disguise his lack of originality: "Indeed, La Fontaine more than others had to look to embellishments, because only these were his own: the inventions and the usage were Aesop's." A true creator, declares Bodmer, exploits the natural beauties of his subject instead of depending on infusions of artificial ornamentation.

Bodmer's "Critical Introduction" turns out to be more assertive than critical. When he tries to be incisive, as in his attempted distinction between "fable catcher" and "fable inventor," he ends up being rather silly. For the most part, it seems best to pass off the introduction as hack work solicited by fabulist or publisher to capitalize on his name.

Bodmer subsequently busied himself with more estimable studies of the fable. At a later date (1757) he collaborated with his literary cohort Breitinger on an edition of the medieval fabulist Ulrich Boner, but his fable ideology always remained substantially independent of Breitinger's. Rather than endorsing the concept of wonder, for example, Bodmer never gives it much credence and typically seems more concerned with the danger of losing the moral instruction in a flight of fantasy. There are, in addition, apparent stylistic and temperamental differences between his writings and Breitinger's. The latter evokes a more sober and theoretical air, even though fits of truculence can land him in contradictions, as noted in reviewing his attack on Triller. Although normally the ideological leader in the collaborations of the duo, Bodmer commonly tends toward journalistic liveliness and frequently seems willing to sacrifice profundity, and even good judgment, for a touch of wit. A game he played by inventing an imaginary fabulist Hermann Axel provides a case in point. He introduced the fictitious fabulist in the periodical *Freimütigen Nachrichten* in 1745 in order to parody Triller, Daniel Stoppe, and other fable writers of the Gottsched faction. In the ninth of his *Kritische Briefe* (*Critical Letters*, 1746) Bodmer contends that his Herr Axel really exists and in the subsequent letter replies to a purported request that he present Herr

Axel's theory of the fable for the benefit of readers. The ideas which he offers, of course, are his own.

Bodmer has his fabulist commence with a description of his own fables: "My fables . . . are nothing other than a noteworthy aspect of a disposition, a tendency, passion, rule of conduct, which I disguise in a little event, a little incident, so that it appears in the deed and the practice, and also becomes quite vivid." [9] In his best freewheeling prose he seems to say that his fables exhibit human qualities and foibles with the intention of instilling virtue by means of the display. The fabulist begins by selecting an aspect of human character or disposition, which is more appropriate if not "too common and ordinary" (p. 164). The second step calls for "a suitable event or merely a significant situation" to illustrate it. The action or situation retains greater naturalness if derived from human life, but it can also be adopted from the animal world without excessively straining observable nature. Although animal personages ensure the additional advantage of wonder, they also increase the danger of making the fable idly fantastic or capricious. The fabulist who avails himself of beasts, therefore, must seek out precise parallels between men and animals.

Herr Axel warns of the difficulties entailed in discovering appropriate parallels, which are limited due to the inherent inferiority of animals: "Their instinct gives out only dark and fleeting glimmers of reason, which do not hold up very long. For this reason fables with animal characters are quite short and consist of only a very simple account or concern. They do not serve to present a human character in more than one aspect; indeed, the fabulist must be content if he can present only one feature of a character" (p. 169). Other theorists have prescribed simplicity in plot and moral; but Herr Axel maintains that simplicity, whether desirable or not, is inevitable with beasts as actors due to the innate shortcomings of animals in human roles. With his inherently uncomplicated nature, an animal can represent little more than a single aspect of the multifaceted human personality. Bodmer returns to the topic in the eleventh of the *Kritische Briefe,* again stressing that the simple, unvaried habits and actions of animals do not lend themselves to forceful depiction of the multifaceted human character.

Herr Axel derides "Le Bossu's" notion that extent comprises the only difference between the Aesopian fable and the epic fable. Le Bossu himself would probably not have objected, however, to ridicule of this misinterpretation of his comparison. Extension of the Aesopian fable, says Herr Axel, tends to humanize the animal characters to such a degree that their behavior becomes farcical and devastating to the moral purpose; the story becomes a mock epic or a comic animal epic, such as *Reineke Fuchs*. Fabulists should restrict animals' insight and their understanding of human activities, in general allowing them no profounder judgments than what their instincts allow.

Although recognizing decisive differences between genres, Axel asserts that the moral intention of the fable coincides with that of epic and tragedy; the primary aim in all three genres is development of character. In regard to moral instruction the genres differ only in extent and complexity, the fable dealing with limited, individual traits and morals, while the greater genres encompass the entire range of the human personality and consider it from various points of view. Fables thus provide an introduction to knowledge, character building, and self-awareness; they open the way to understanding of man and of the world in general, or what Herr Axel calls "knowledge of the way of the world" (p. 180). Without the moral lesson, however, the fable offers nothing more than "a story out of natural history" (p. 182).

Herr Axel boasts that he has invented a novel variety of fable in which animals relate stories touching on the world of men. The variation necessitates elevating the capabilities of animals to allow profounder insights on their part, but the increased potential to shame people compensates for this disadvantage. The innovation is not as great as Axel believes. Earlier works have endowed animals with the power of insight into human nature, for example, Dryden's *The Hind and the Panther*—and most particularly the fable of the birds in the third part of that work. Herr Axel furnishes examples of his own to illustrate his new variety; but Samuel Johnson's "Fable of the Vultures," written some fifteen years later,[10] most memorably demonstrates the formula. In Johnson's fable a mother vulture explains the ways of the world to her young, quoting the opinion of a wise old vulture in order to derive a modicum of sense from the enigmatic activities of the species called man. The explanation develops into a misanthropic condemnation of the human race, focused on the absurdities of war.

In the eleventh of the *Kritische Briefe* Bodmer praises the collection *Fables for the Female Sex* (1744) by the Englishman Edward Moore. His sole unfavorable criticism concerns their undue complexity. Bodmer suggests that many would be more effective with human or allegorical personages rather than bestial—his notion, once again, about the limitations of animal characters. Moore himself, in the preface to his collection, refuses to take his fables seriously and declares them to be intended for idle amusement: "As they are the writings of an idle hour, so they are intended for the reading of those, whose only business is amusement." [11] Bodmer, however, contradicts Moore's own statement, evidently considering it a product of modest or of a droll sense of humor, and asserts that the fabulist actually had an unswerving moral aim: "but one well recognizes that his secret aim, in the midst of the amusement, is to teach useful rules, how a female, in a manner becoming her sex, can arrange her life for her greater well-being and enjoyment." [12] If Bodmer is right, Moore adopted a subtle—even sneaky—approach to moral instruction.

Despite Bodmer's insistence upon moral purpose, many fables throughout the eighteenth century were written with little educational intent or with mere lip service paid to it. There is no reason not to take Moore at his word, especially since the whimsical fable comprises a considerable portion of the English tradition; and one might even grant him credit for being more honest than many of his fellow fabulists. But even German fabulists did not always take the genre seriously. Johann Wilhelm Gleim's fables, for example, include many emanating a humorous tone, such as the one which introduces the second part of his collection and which scarcely establishes a mood for serious moral instruction. ''The traveling fable'' speaks:

> ''Ah!'' she said, ''Madam, I am,
> I know it well, nothing but a pastime;
> Only children willingly hear me.
> Teach people? Far be it from me!
> That duty falls to priests and wise men.
> They must do the instruction.[13]

   Through various of his *Critical Letters* Bodmer thus formulates the view of the fable as a kind of primer for building character, a purpose which it accomplishes by teaching rudimentary morals and elementary knowledge of man and the world. The more complex literary genres, tragedy and epic, take up the educational function where the fable leaves off. Bodmer repeatedly warns about the limitations of animal characters, although he ignores his own warnings when he describes his ''innovative'' fable—using animals to make observations about man. He implies that fabulists could circumvent this limitation by adopting human characters, but at the same time he seems to accept animals as the normal actors in the fable. The undrawn conclusion would seem to be that the fable is by nature a limited form. Hence, its function as pedagogical primer. In any case, Bodmer's discussion in the *Critical Letters* leaves us with a serious, edifying conception of the fable. Bodmer will return in Chapter VII, when he answers Lessing's fables and theory with parodies and further ideas of his own.

   After singing the praises of Meyer von Knonau's fables in the ''Critical Introduction'' to the volume discussed above, Bodmer concludes with a flourish of Swiss nationalism. He commends the fabulist for composing in the *Swiss* language rather than resorting to the ''Leipzig dialect'' (modern High German). Christian Fürchtegott Gellert, writing in the same year, critically considers Meyer von Knonau's fables among others composed in the *German* language and concludes that the reader of this collection will remain perplexed as to why the author of the "Introduction"—Bodmer—waxed so enthusiastic about it.[14]

Gellert speaks with considerable authority. At the University of Leipzig, first as student and later as professor, Gellert sided with those who rejected Gottsched's classical pedantry. He subsequently gained renown as teacher, charming personality, and writer in various genres, including a novel, *The Swedish Countess von G.* (1746), which imitates Richardson's *Pamela.* With his poetry, including spiritual songs and fables, Gellert achieved a popularity second to none in eighteenth-century Germany, although the enduring estimate of his work does not measure up to that contemporary popularity. Whatever the esthetic grounds for the modern, more sceptical assessment, however, it must also be kept in mind that Gellert's poetry is invariably didactic, which suited eighteenth-century tastes but which does not set well in the twentieth.

His fables began appearing in 1741 in the periodical *Belustigungen des Verstandes und des Witzes;* a collected edition was published in 1746 and later expanded. According to Frederick the Great, for whatever its critical worth, Gellert's fables rank as the finest poetry in the German language up to Frederick's time of writing (1780). Considered in context, however, his estimate seems less a recommendation than a narrow escape from condemnation. Frederick's *De la Littérature allemande* is a patronizing discussion of the barbarities of his countrymen and subjects. While admitting the existence of first-rate German philosophers. Frederick discovers no superior practitioners of the belles-lettres: "All that I can grant you without making myself the vile flatterer of my compatriots is that in the little genre of fables we have had a Gellert, who established himself at the side of Phaedrus and Aesop." [15]

Gellert also drafted a series of essays, *Abhandlungen von den Fabeln und deren Verfasser (Essays on Fables and Their Authors);* the original Latin version was submitted to the University of Leipzig in 1744 to qualify him for a professorship. (The German version was published in 1772, three years after Gellert's death.) His essays taken

together comprise one of the most comprehensive theoretical works on
the fable, although much of his material constitutes an eclectic composite of borrowed ideas rather than an original contribution. He ex-
tracts from La Motte, Breitinger, Gottsched, and others but, to do him
justice, frequently expands and clarifies what they only suggest. On
occasion, however, Gellert slips into apparent ambiguity; for example,
his definition: "A short fiction which alludes to a certain subject and
which is arranged so that it delights at the same time that it
profits." [16] This definition seems to specify the Aesopian fable; but a
footnote refers to various genres of fables, such as Gottsched discussed in his *Versuch einer critischen Dichtkunst*. Gellert declines to
undertake a discussion of them, "because they are different more in
name than in fact." At another point he alludes to the "large fables"—tragedy and epic—but shortly thereafter construes the fable as
"a foreshortened epic" (p. 17), noting his agreement with La Motte
and Breitinger. Gellert also calls Boccaccio's *Decameron* a collection
of fables, although admitting that they focus on amusement rather than
instruction (pp. 84–85). In any case, neither tragedy nor epic nor Boccaccio's *Decameron* correspond to Gellert's definition of the fable as
quoted above. He apparently has both the broader and narrower meanings of the term in mind, but the bulk of his discussion unmistakably
concerns the *Aesopian* fable.

For Gellert, the essential quality of a fable is imaginative invention. He admits that such stress of imagination has been disputed by
critics who prefer to emphasize the instructional purpose and who,
therefore, strive to remain as close as possible to "truth," both in the
definition and creation of the fable. Gellert claims, however, that
"uninvented" fables are rare exceptions. This clarification also implies the possibility of fables without invention, however rare they
might be, even though Gellert previously singled out this quality as the
essence of the genre. He proceeds, nevertheless, to distinguish between *fable* and *history* (*Geschichte*): the latter resembles the former if
it relates something marvelous or strange but fails to qualify as a fable
unless it be at least partially invented. According to this distinction an

uninvented fable is a history and not a fable at all. The attempted differentiation results in confusion rather than clarification. As Bodmer previously noted, moreover, the reader has no way of knowing how, or even whether, the fable was invented. Compounding the confusion about invention and fable, Gellert also mentions story (*Erzählung*), which "contains nothing but what all men know and see; therefore it will scarcely delight" (p. 17). He does not explain what difference, if any, he perceives between a story and a history.

Assuming that the fable must reflect imagination and consequently arouse a degree of wonder, Gellert delineates three situations or conditions that effect it: 1) "something contrary to daily experience, which indeed can happen but which does not often happen"; 2) something possible only through divine intervention; or, 3) something conceivable after the acceptance of certain stipulations, such as speaking animals (p. 31). The latter two situations derive from the Ancients and concern, respectively, classical mythology and traditional belief in a primeval period when animals could speak. Poetic license and universal familiarity ensure their acceptance and ready comprehension by Moderns. Wonder does not derive, however, simply from endowing dumb beasts with the power of speech, but rather from "when they undertake something unexpected and great with those powers" (p. 33). Gellert explains that it frequently arises from a plot skillfully joining lesser circumstances which in themselves contain nothing out of the ordinary.

Warning that *improbable* occurrences but not *impossible* ones excite wonder, Gellert echoes La Motte, Breitinger, and other predecessors by prescribing a solid foundation of plausibility. For actors he prefers animals, plants, and concrete things, which contain inherent roots of plausibility, rather than pagan gods and spirits, which depend on erroneous beliefs of former ages. In adapting the natural material to a fable, moreover, the fabulist "beautifies but does not alter the animals and things." Normally mute creatures converse but utter only what is compatible with their essential natures; they behave reasonably but retain their inherent traits. On the other hand, the characters cannot remain exactly true to their natures: "Who would get excited by something that he sees daily?" (pp. 25–27). The fable, therefore, contains a blend of nature and invention, of plausibility and wonder. The pleasure which the fable arouses comes from this resemblance but difference between animals and man, a relationship which Gellert likens to that of a painting with its model. Excessive humanization destroys this artistic relationship and, consequently, the delight to be derived from it. Furthermore, the fable's teaching effectiveness gains much of its strength from the unstated observation that lowly animals frequently behave themselves with greater virtue and intelligence than man, who haughtily scorns them. Humanization of the animals destroys this sobering comparison and thereby depletes the value of the fable. Gellert provides two examples, one a fable from Aesop in which a wolf thinks and speaks but still comports himself like a wolf, a second from La Motte in which two doves behave like a pair of silly young girls and are birds only in name. The first illustration demonstrates the proper perspective for a fable, whereas the second confuses the animal and human levels and results in a deficiency of both plausibility and wonder.

Like his predecessors, Gellet has much to say concerning the didactic element. A suitable blend of art and instruction is difficult to achieve, he declares, but indispensable: "Nothing can be taught completely without art nor completely through art" (p. 35). Since the fabulist must leave the moral impressed on the reader's mind rather than the incident which illustrates it, the incident must lead unswervingly to the moral lesson, which, in turn, must arise naturally and unmistakably from the portrayed action. To effectuate the educational purpose, both fable and moral must be simple (*einfach*); the fable should contain neither more nor less material than the basic moral purpose demands. Either excessive or insufficient material may cause the moral lesson to go awry, in which case the reader encounters an amusing story and nothing more. There is no reason, nevertheless, to restrict a fable to a single moral, provided the fabulist ensures the unity of the plot. A separate, explicit moral tag, in any case, should conclude the fable, since even the apparently most lucid ones contain potential ambiguities. If readers discover the proposed lesson on their own, before arriving at the appended tag, it pleases them to find their perceptions verified: "it is almost as pleasing to them as if they had invented the matter themselves" (p. 43). An attached exegesis carried to excessive length or obviousness, however, bores the reader or insults his intelligence.

Although the fabulist as a general rule should avoid digressions, tasteful external decoration has an integral function. Gellert includes in this decorative category artistic touches that elevate the narrative to the realm of poetry, such as attractive descriptions and clever exaggerations. The fabulist should ascertain, however, that the additional beauty and pleasure compensate for the detriment of extended length. Properly executed, these embellishments, which demonstrate the genuine art of the fabulist, serve "to extend the fable and, in a suitable way, to hold the reader back and make him curious about what comes next" (p. 45). Embellishments create suspense, serving essentially the same purpose in the fable as in the epic. The epic poet, typically beginning with subject matter no more extensive than the fabulist's, creatively stretches it to epic length with such contrivances as episodes, speeches, and descriptions. Gellert declares that ancient fabulists tended to avoid artistic adornment, to adhere to stark plot and moral, whereas their contemporary successors skillfully weave poetical embellishment into the essential narrative. La Fontaine, La Motte, and Hagedorn merit his particular commendation. He warns poetically-oriented modern fabulists, however, to remain faithful to the "dry and frosty style" (p. 53) of the genre and declares that the artistic ornamentation must derive from the fable itself, rather than be superimposed like a foreign object. However commendable their esthetic efforts might be, modern fabulists occasionally abandon the essential fable and ·dedicate themselves entirely to the invention of lavish poetical trimmings. Concluding this section of his treatise with advice on maintaining a proper balance between originality and tradition, Gellert asserts that a fabulist, or any poet, should avoid rigid obedience to established form but, on the other hand, should consult "perceptive and honest judges of true beauty" (p. 55). He holds to the middle of the road, as usual, steering clear of committing himself to one extreme or the other.

Describing the fable in the by now familiar terms of "a pleasing lesson," Gellert admits that the genre occasionally attracts deprecation because it speaks to youths and common people rather than to the learned. In reply he asserts that the contribution to juvenile education in itself proves the worth of the genre and cites Plato's approval of it, even though Plato would ban all other literature from his Republic. But fables also admirably serve adults, e.g., "the female sex and all who, though not learned, love well-being." They instruct by means of images rather than abstract concepts and, therefore, enable everyone, of whatever class, sex, or educational accomplishment, to perceive "what is true, just, equitable, beautiful, and decent" (p. 57). Dramatic comedy served the Ancients to instruct the masses, a service which it no longer renders; and the fable has assumed this vital pedagogical task.

The last of Gellert's essays is a critical survey of fabulists. He eulogizes La Fontaine's artistic achievement while appreciating La Motte's distinction of being the first to approach the Aesopian fable critically. Gellert views with scepticism the accomplishments of most modern fabulists—for example, Hagedorn is the sole contemporary German to merit his unqualified praise—but he reserves his sternest judgments for his own fables. In 1756, twelve years after the *Abhandlungen* and fifteen after his own fables began appearing in the periodical *Belustigungen des Verstandes und des Witzes,* Gellert drafted a *Beurteilungen einiger Fabeln aus den Belustigungen* (*Criticism of Some Fables out of the "Belustigungs"*), for which he selected three of his own fables and subjected them to a line-by-line critical analysis. His judgment is harsh: the story fails to harmonize with the moral; the style is forced, discursive, and prosaic; the rime lacks control; the necessary moral is obscure or missing. The overall tenor of his unrelenting criticism suggests Gellert's movement toward a more ascetic concept of the fable—demanding an incisive moral and excluding adornment—similar to that which Lessing would prescribe three years later. Gellert explains the rigorous critique of his own work as the result of a sincere desire to provide a lesson in critical judgment for beginning poets, in addition to an aversion to mediocrity. He concludes, however, that even after correction of the indicated errors the fables would still be mediocre.

In general, Gellert's essays provide a thorough and balanced treatment of the fable. If his terminology and explanations at times become confused, he never runs off the track of logic in order to pummel a rival, as does Breitinger, nor does his discussion ever stumble into the occasional silliness of Bodmer's. His personality does not seem inclined to either diatribe or flippancy. Gellert builds his concept of the fable around the idea of wonder, as do Triller and Breitinger, balanced by plausible adherence to nature. Most theories of the fable formulated during the century require, in one form or another, this balance of nature and imagination, of art and instruction. Gellert's definition, "an agreeable lesson," derives from predecessors, as does the comparison with the epic; and both passed through other hands before arriving in his. Gellert provides no ideological revelations nor even any significant deviations from orthodoxy; but his treatment of the genre develops a comprehensible synthesis of ideas drawn from his predecessors and common to his contemporaries.

CHAPTER SIX

French Ideas at Mid-Century

Two of the writers discussed in this chapter, Batteux and Marmontel, were literary critics and theoreticians; both treated the fable within the framework of larger works encompassing literature in general. The third, the Abbé Aubert, composed fables; and his critical comments supplement his own creations. Although none of the three effected a revolution in the genre, new points of view emanate from their works, such as Marmontel's emphasis on naiveté and good faith as the sublime qualities of a successful fabulist. All three venerate La Fontaine, the pride of the Moderns and, in their opinion, the successful challenger of Aesop and Phaedrus to become undisputed master fabulist. They accord La Motte respectable consideration, although not the reverence granted La Fontaine, and agree that discussion of fables and fabulists necessitates attention to these two key figures before considering any others.

Charles Batteux published his *Beaux Arts réduits à un même principe* in 1746 and *Cours de belles-lettres,* an introduction to literature primarily for young people, in 1763. The two works subsequently appeared together as *Principes de la littérature.* The earlier treatise synthesizes, as the title indicates, whereas the latter volume dissects each genre separately in order to analyze and define its component parts.

In *Beaux Arts réduits* Batteux stresses the instructive foundation upon which all poetry is built. The assorted genres present varied facades, each designed to please a specific audience; but all have the same didactic foundation: "Wisdom, with the help of poetry, takes all the forms necessary to insinuate herself; and as tastes are different, according to age and situation, she is willing to play with children; she laughs with the people; speaks royally with kings; and thus she distributes her lessons to all men; she joins the agreeable to the useful in order to draw to her all those who love nothing but pleasure and in order to reward those who have no other aim but to improve themselves." [1] The fable is the genre designed for children; or, in Batteux's words, it presents "le Spectacle des Enfans" (I, 292). It differs from the other genres solely in the actors which it employs: "In this little theater one sees neither Alexanders nor Caesars, but the fly and the ant, who perform as men in their own way" (I, 292). The fable presents a comedy which avoids subtleties and complications in order to radiate a brighter instructive light than other genres.

Batteux emphasizes that creation of a fable proceeds according to the same rules that govern epic and tragedy. The characters vary, but the moral and social significance of their actions remains constant in each genre: the frog who puffs himself up with pride and finally bursts is appropriate for the fable; the social-climbing bourgeois gentlemen for the comedy; and the ambitious Caesar for the epic. Each plot outline, although geared to the tastes and understanding of a distinct age-group or social level, illustrates the same lesson; collectively, the various literary genres provide for the edification of everybody. If there is a characteristic peculiar to the fable alone, it derives from the fabulist's traditional liberty to endow everything in the universe with the power of speech. The inventors of the genre first conceded the verbal gift to animals, who bear the closest relationship to man, then to plants, which also live, and finally to the innumerable inanimate things that comprise the universe. The vast potential for characterization excludes, however, purely spiritual beings or ideas; the difficulties of furnishing them with body and vitalizing them in an action tend to be insurmountable. Batteux thus eliminates pure allegory from the fable, although he, like most of his countrymen, defines the genre as an allegorical form.

Like epic and dramatic poetry the fable must include an action with beginning, end, and conflict. Although its non-human actors imitate the ways of men, Batteux subscribes to the usual requirement that they still conform to their own inherent natures. By way of example, he analyzes the fable of the wolf and the lamb, in which the wolf, blending native rapaciousness and human subtlety, advances a variety of spurious justifications for doing what he fully intends to do anyway, that is, devour the lamb. Concluding that the fable demonstrates the cruelty that accompanies injustice and excites in its own way both terror and pity, Batteux calls it a tragedy in miniature.

Despite this accentuation of the didactic element in *Beaux Arts réduits,* Batteux commences his later work, *Cours de belles-lettres,* with a comprehensive definition of the arts which omits mention of instructive purpose: "all the fine arts, at the head of which is poetry, have no other object but to imitate nature, each in its own distinctive manner, in order to excite in us agreeable sentiments." [2] Nor does delineation of the qualities of the fable bring forth any declaration of moral purpose: "The apologue, also called the fable, is the account of an allegorical action, ordinarily ascribed to animals" (II, 3). Batteux proceeds to analyze the components of the genre by carefully defining the key words used in the definition. The fable is an *account* (*récit*), which means that it *tells about* events instead of *describing* them, "as the spectacle does." Batteux's opinion seems to have undergone a change since the previous treatise, in which he continually drew the parallel between fable and drama, even depicting the former as "the spectacle for children." Nor, as noted below, does he now limit its appeal to children.

The fable is an account, but more specifically an account of an action, an enterprise accomplished with choice and purpose as opposed to a fortuitous event. The action, moreover, is allegorical, transmitting a concealed moral truth. The fable should combine clarity and brevity and should avoid both trivialities and metaphysical complexities. Batteux divides the genre into the three categories—reasonable, moral, and mixed—previously used to classify fables in the general sense. And in regard to style: "simple, familiar, cheerful, graceful, natural, and even naive" (II, 13).

Batteux traces the origins of the fable to prehistoric times, postulating that primitive man, possessing few words, expressed himself with images and comparisons. Hence the birth of allegory. Its advantages perceived, allegory was adapted to the teaching of morality. The use of animals in order to avoid the resentment that direct instruction of human examples arouse is by no means subtle, declares Batteux, and betrays the primitive source of the fable. But the device continues to be eminently effective even in sophisticated societies. Batteux's derivation of the genre from primitive times represents no innovation in itself—Addison, for one, had remarked its venerability fifty years earlier—but it is a notion that assumes increasing importance in the latter half of the eighteenth century.

To conclude his chapter on the fable, Batteux provides a critical description of the most prominent fabulists, among whom La Fontaine reigns supreme. Batteux ranks him with Corneille, Racine, and Molière and eulogizes his timeless appeal for people of all ages and conditions of life: "He is the toy of children, the mentor of youth, the friend of the grown man" (II, 44). His fables provide a moral treatise for the philosopher, a perfect model of good taste for the man of letters, and a portrait of society for the man of the world. Since La Motte's turn for consideration comes immediately following this lavish praise, it is not surprising that the lesser fabulist suffers comparative disparagement. La Motte's fables, remarks Batteux, "have made so much noise in the world, that it is necessary to say a word about them here" (II, 72). He graciously, if perfunctorily, gives La Motte credit for a commendable output but denies him more than an occasional glimmer of La Fontaine's sublime radiance.

Batteux's discussion of fables in his earlier *Beaux Arts réduits à un même principe* provides a clear, orderly synthesis of standard classical ideas. Like all the arts, literature aims to make instruction pleasing, which is the single underlying principle the title refers to. The various genres exist in order to reach people of all ages and from all walks of life. The fable aims at children and thus simplifies the lesson and delivers it through the mouths of beasts, a ploy designed to catch the fancy of the youthful audience.

In the later work, however, Batteux includes in his definitions
nothing at all about instruction; and the objective he ascribes to the
arts—to excite agreeable sentiments—could even be construed as an
art-for-art's-sake esthetic. It is only when he discusses the primitive
origins of the fable that he brings in the moral purpose of at least this
genre.

Beyond this contradiction, two points in Batteux's later treatment
deserve note. One is the already remarked attention to the fable's
primitive past. Although Batteux sees the primitive lack of subtlety as
a possible detriment to its pedagogical effectiveness in a more sophisticated world, later commentators look upon the primitive origin as a
virtue and discover in the fable mysteries out of a legendary past. The
second point is the lofty praise of La Fontaine. Instead of portraying
the skillful poet of the Age of Reason, it hints at the inspired genius of
the Romantics. Beginning with this perceptible shift in tone, eventually the point is reached where the fabulist needs an inspirational spark
more than he needs a cogent moral lesson and knowledge of rules and
models to show him how to make a fable out of it.

The hints become stronger with Jean François Marmontel, whose
general appraisals of both La Fontaine and La Motte resemble Batteux's. As Marmontel perceives it the essential difference between the
two fabulists appears to be genius, which, to state it bluntly, La Fontaine possessed and La Motte lacked.

Marmontel's article "Fable, *apologue*" in his *Élémens de littérature* (1787) had served earlier as the entry "Fable" in the *En-
cyclopédie* (1751–1765), and the *Élémens* itself follows the orderly
method of an encyclopedia. In developing his discussion Marmontel
immediately brings in both La Motte and La Fontaine. The former's
insights into the fable in his "Discourse," he declares, are admirably
pondered and formulated; and his prescribed rules are just. But the
qualities and precepts which La Motte sets forth produce, when combined, no more than a *"fable régulière,"* which falls considerably
short of excellence. La Motte's criticism of La Fontaine is also justified, as far as it goes. Even La Fontaine's worst fables, nevertheless,

radiate a charm and excite an interest—no matter how many rules they break—alien to La Motte's most regular ones. La Fontaine's artistic superiority derives from a combination of qualities, but foremost is "the naiveté of narrative and of style, the dominant characteristic of La Fontaine's genius." Esteeming naiveté as the supreme asset of a fabulist, moreover, Marmontel quotes Batteux's description of fable style—"simple, familiar, cheerful, graceful, natural, and even naive"—and corrects it to "above all naive." [3]

Since poetic naiveté assumes such importance, Marmontel defines and explains the quality at length. It signifies more than just simplicity or candor or innocence. When moral purity accompanies simplicity, the result is *candor;* innocence added to candor gives *ingenuousness;* and if the ingenuousness displays qualities which self-interest might have advised disguising and thereby gaining an advantage over others, the result is *naiveté* or "naive ingenuousness" (VII, 372). Marmontel quotes La Motte, who traced the success of the fable to the fact that the allegory coddles and flatters the ego. Marmontel agrees and identifies this quality as naiveté: "that manner of pampering and flattering the ego, instead of wounding it, is nothing else but naive eloquence, the eloquence of Aesop among the Ancients and of La Fontaine among the Moderns" (VII, 373).

Of all human pretensions and vanities, continues Marmontel, the most prevalent concern wisdom and morals. Attempts to develop wisdom and to inculcate morality invariably incur the danger of running aground on the rocky shallows of the human ego. Poetry, therefore, disguises instruction under an agreeable and interesting action. The greater genres, such as epic and drama, are undeniably more impressive but also suffer limitations; drama, for example, is "a public mirror" which requires money and machines to set up. In order to provide a mobile alternative to the cumbersome epic and drama, poets invented fables, "portable looking glasses, just as accurate and more convenient, where each isolated truth has its distinct image" (VII, 375).

Fables may employ as actors either people, supernatural beings, or personified plants and animals; but the latter category has consistently seen most extensive use. Marmontel suggests, moreover, that it might possibly result in the only genuine fable, simply because plants and animals least resemble us. Distance from human reality is important. Instruction or correction by a fellow human being invariably arouses resistance, stemming from the suspicion that the instructor considers himself superior to his pupils. The fabulist avoids this problem by playfully calling on animals, distinctly inferior to us, so that one accepts the truth "like so many traits of naiveté without consequence" (VII, 376). The persuasive power of the fable thus lies firmly embedded in naiveté, which lulls the human ego into nonresistance and thereby allows the moral lesson smoothly to inculcate itself.

Marmontel declares that it requires an exceptional man convincingly to relate a fable: "a man simple enough and credulous enough to repeat seriously the childish stories that have been told to him; and the naiveté of narrative or of style consists of this air of good faith" (VII, 378). If related without the air of sincerity and good faith, the fable either remains a childish tale or degenerates into a parody or burlesque. No one, he maintains, infuses and transmits the air of *bonne foi* better than La Fontaine. Aesop tells his fables simply, seeming to repeat what he has heard; but La Fontaine manages to appear an eyewitness of the action. His air of sincerity and good faith are such that "one is tempted to cry out at each instant, 'the *bonhomme!*' " (VII, 380). The *bonhomme* creates to perfection the air of *bonne foi,* injecting seriousness into little things and, with absolute good faith, juxtaposing and blending them with great things. This blending results in the allegory or illusion on which the fable depends.

Marmontel delineates three fundamental rules for a fabulist: first, the fabulist himself must appear persuaded of everything he says; second, he must transmit his persuasion under an amusing guise; third, he must extract utility from the amusement. Since the first step of the procedure underlies the other two, Marmontel stresses that the fabulist's primary aim should not be to persuade readers that lions and wolves and other creatures are talking and reasoning but to seem per-

suaded of it himself. This "credulity of the narrator" is vital to the
success of the fable. Success also demands reasonable adherence to
nature, in the sense that animals and other characters must abide by
their inherent traits; but the fable unavoidably transcends nature by endowing mute creatures with the human characteristics of speech and
reason. This aspect of the fable—the "fabulous" element—demands
the good faith and credulity of the narrator.

The fable amuses but above all instructs—the third and ultimate
concern of the fabulist. It should conclude with the development of
some useful truth, and Marmontel emphasizes *développement* as opposed to *preuve*. The fable proves nothing. It is an example, a particular act which illustrates a universal moral; but the moral itself must be
known beforehand for the reader to recognize it in the example and be
persuaded of its validity. The fable does not effect a conversion, nor
inspire a moral revelation, nor even convince. It administers a warning: "The example contained in the fable is the indication of it and not
the proof: its aim is to warn, not to convince; and its function is to
make perceptible to the imagination that which the reason avows"
(VII, 393). The fable encourages the active function of a known truth.
Initial attraction of the reader's attention requires an amusing exterior,
but the reader still must be led unswervingly to the moral truth. Marmontel commends La Motte for the directness of his moral aim, noting
that La Fontaine sometimes neglects it.

In the subsequent section of *Élémens de littérature,* the article
"Fable, *composition poëtique,*" Marmontel discusses fable in the
broader sense but confines his treatment to the plot of epic or drama
rather than including all narrative. He also differentiates among *fable,
action,* and *subject,* although admitting that they are frequently accepted as synonyms. In addition to redefining the broader significance
of the term "fable" so that it embraces a narrower scope than that ordinarily assigned to it in the seventeenth century, Marmontel also
refutes the notion that a poet properly begins with a moral and subsequently invents a fable to illustrate it: the poet, on the contrary,
typically creates the fable first, except "in little poems like the apo-

logue" (VII, 399). The *Iliad* affirms a truth identical to the one illustrated in some of Aesop's fables, and the action of both the epic and the Aesopian fables is fundamentally the same. It would be misguided, however, to claim that Homer first contemplated a truth and then referred to the Trojan War in order to illustrate it. He obviously had the heroic conflict in mind first.

Marmontel thus denies the *exclusively* moral basis of poetry, in the sense that the poet thinks of a moral precept before undertaking invention of the plot. Literature remains rooted in morality, but Marmontel's interpretation depicts the poet as extracting a moral lesson from whatever story he chooses to relate. Only the fable and kindred didactic forms demand that the poet proceed with an initial moral in mind. The fable, therefore, no longer flows with the mainstream of literature. In former days it merely intensified the didacticism expected of all literary genres. Now it retains its didactic foundation while critical opinion requires for the majority of genres a structure based on inspiring events and imaginative creation.

Marmontel's discussion, moreover, significantly emphasizes naiveté and good faith over rules. Rules continue to be imperative; but La Motte, no matter how carefully he orders his fables by them, cannot compete with La Fontaine, the superlative *bonhomme*. The comparison and terminology unavoidably suggest the effusive man of natural genius as opposed to the disciplined man of reason who faithfully adheres to the logic of rules. Marmontel's naiveté, furthermore, approaches in meaning Schiller's conception of the same term in "On Naive and Sentimental Poetry": spontaneous, "natural" expression as opposed to reasoned, artificial expression. As we shall see, the advantages of naiveté, spontaneity, and uncontrived naturalness for a fabulist become increasingly recognized and predicated throughout the rest of the century.

The third figure to be considered briefly in this chapter, the Abbé Jean-Louis Aubert, served as professor of French literature, director of the *Royal Gazette,* and royal censor; and he remained a member in good standing and staunch defender of the *ancien régime*. Even his fables, which first appeared in 1756, vigorously assail the Philosophes and the stream of radical ideas which flowed through the Paris salons. Aubert assumes a progressive stance, on the other hand, in regard to artistic originality: "Servile imitation is not natural, and the timid aim of restricting oneself to it is ordinarily the germ of mediocrity. There have never been any of true fame in the arts except those who have had the ambition to be original and the courage to become it." [4] He commends La Motte for striking out on his own and attributes the failure of La Fontaine's emulators to their lack of any purpose but servile imitation. Nor is even the master himself excluded from the rebuke: La Fontaine's sublimest creations by far are those fables in which he sought originality rather than those in which he translated word for word from Phaedrus. [5]

Aubert nevertheless exalts La Fontaine's poetic accomplishments. Quoting from his fables, he asserts that nothing comparable exists in all of French poetry and stresses, at the same time, that fables—and especially La Fontaine's—are *poetry*. Although the French master sometimes elicits criticism for not being comprehensible to children, Aubert replies that, far from being a fault, his sophistication indicates his poetic eminence.

Aubert proceeds to outline the qualities that a superior fabulist must possess: naïveté of narrative style, delicacy of thought, philosophical gaiety in the moral, exquisite sense of choice in imagery, an air of good faith, apparent simplicity. Some of these qualities we have just seen delineated by Marmontel; others describe in general the gifted poet rather than the fabulist in particular. Assessing La Motte by these standards, Aubert finds him lacking in poetic qualities and labels him a philosopher rather than a poet. His fables, although skillfully invented, want grace, taste, and other refinements of distinguished poetry. The accomplishments of his incomparable predecessor La Fontaine, however, hampered La Motte. A poet who works in a genre overshadowed by a revered genius either tends to produce mere imitations or, if he succeeds in abiding by the dictates of his own talent, to suffer rejection by a public attuned to the tradition established by the reigning genius—that is, to be criticized for *not* imitating. Aubert condemns this negative attitude as destructive to literature and to progress in general. The fable offers greater potential than usually imagined, he maintains; and no one should feel inhibited about trying his hand at it nor feel constrained to imitate. The battle against vice, moreover, must be unceasingly waged, for which the fable provides an excellent weapon. Aubert's pointed encouragement of would-be fabulists arouses the suspicion that he seeks to counteract adverse attitudes, undoubtedly emanating from critics who remark the high quality of La Fontaine's accomplishment, the limitations of the genre, and the redundancy or relative futility of further attempts in it. At the time that Aubert writes, the fable still maintains the peak of its popularity. Negative comments can be shrugged off as the perversity of chronic disparagers. In ensuing years, however, comments on the futility of producing additional fables become increasingly numerous and the cries of the defenders of the genre increasingly shrill.

CHAPTER SEVEN

Lessing's Aesopian Fables and the Anti-Lessing

By any estimate Gotthold Ephraim Lessing ranks as one of the major figures of eighteenth-century German literature and letters. Author of historically important and still staged plays, his enduring fame probably rests more heavily on his works of criticism and esthetics, which mark the turn from the classical tradition to the modern. To a great extent Lessing personifies the Enlightenment in Germany. He preached tolerance, welcomed new ideas, and helped pave the way for the brilliant period of Goethe, Schiller, and the Romantics.

Such was one side of Lessing. On the other side, he was stern, didactic, and dedicated to discipline and the inculcation of unadorned morality. On this side obtrudes Lessing the representative and product of German protestantism and the advocate of rule and order. This harsher side of Lessing is the one which pervades his discussion of fables. Indeed, he takes his predecessors and contemporaries to task, the theoreticians for inaccuracy, the fabulists for burying the moral lesson under poetic fluff. The result is a methodical, incisive analysis of the fable, accompanied by a rather stark depiction of it as a didactic tool, stripped of extraneous ornament or poetic play.

Among his multiple literary concerns Lessing maintained a life-long interest in the fable; he composed both fables of his own and essays on the genre. In the preface to one of his collections he confesses his fascination with the genre and provides a partial explanation for it: ''With no genre of poetry had I tarried longer than with the

fable. This common border of poetry and moral pleased me." [1] He
declares, furthermore, that he had extensively studied the genre before
undertaking his own theoretical treatment.

Lessing began publishing his fables in 1747, and he collected the
output of the next few years under the title *Fabeln und Erzählungen in
Reimen* (*Fables and Stories in Rime*) for inclusion in his *Schriften* of
1753. Gellert and La Fontaine serve him as models in these fables,
many of which are satirical, even caustic, and some of which involve
themselves in contemporary literary polemics. "The Sparrow and the
Fieldmouse," for example, ridicules the imitators of Friedrich Gottlieb
Klopstock; and "The Sun," striking out at Gottsched and his followers, defends Klopstock and his poetic innovations against their vit-
riolic criticism. All of the fables in this early collection employ rime;
and Lessing infuses them with grace and charm, even when his intentions incline toward fierce satire.

Lessing's style and form undergo an abrupt change in *Fabeln:
Drei Bücher,* published six years later in 1759. In these fables he
strictly eschews rime and other poetic accoutrements in favor of ascetic prose and substitutes a stern moral purpose for the satire and polemics which characterized the earlier ones. By this time Lessing has
rejected La Fontaine, Gellert, and others of the school of fabulist who
sought to infuse poetry into the genre. He undertakes what amounts to
a puritan reform and campaigns for a return to the Aesopian prototype,
as he sees it—the pure, unadulterated fable, short, direct, strictly
moral, and devoid of poetic decorations or distractions. A series of
five *Abhandlungen* (*Essays*), each of which discusses an aspect of the
fable, accompanies his 1759 collection; together the five essays
present Lessing's theory of the genre and constitute the critical basis
for his reform movement.

At the outset of the first essay, "On the Essence of the Fable,"
Lessing makes clear that "fable" specifically designates the Aesopian
fable. He proceeds methodically to develop his own definition of the
genre by quoting, analyzing, and correcting previous definitions.
Beginning with La Motte's "the fable is an instruction disguised under

the allegory of an action," Lessing first criticizes the failure of this definition to consider the narrative aspect: the fable is "not only an allegorical action but the *narrative* of such an action" (v, 157). Second, he rejects the notion of allegory, which says something different from what it seems to say and implies a relationship no closer than similarity. The fable, on the other hand, *is* what it represents: "not similar, but *is* or *equals*" (v, 159). Lessing seems to demand a realistic case history—he uses the term "true events" (v, 154)—for the ideal fable rather than an imaginary or hypothetical situation, although in view of the animals, plants, and inanimate objects which the fable employs as characters it is difficult to perceive how this "realism" can have more than relative application. Lessing, however, does recognize two kinds of fables: simple (*einfache*), which function on a single, non-allegorical level; and complex (*zusammengesetzte*), which are allegorical. He unmistakably prefers the former, claiming that Aesop's own creations belong to it. Thus, even though initially rejecting the idea of allegorical fables, he does ultimately, if grudgingly, admit their existence. He then adds, however, that a "merely allegorical" fable is inadequate—and not an authentic fable at all (v, 162). The relationship of allegory to the fable remains a confusing point throughout Lessing's discussion. He unmistakably eliminates *pure* allegory, such as the personification of abstract qualities; but the mere use of animals and other non-human characters, all of them endowed with speech, reason, and other human attributes, suggests that allegory is an unavoidable element of the fable.

Lessing finds fault with one other point in La Motte's definition. It is not sufficient merely to designate instruction as the purpose of the fable: the instruction must be moral.

Turning next to Richer's definition of the fable as "a small poem which contains a precept hidden under an allegorical image," Lessing recognizes an attempt to improve on La Motte's definition but denies success. "Poem" implies "a mere fiction," which incorrectly describes the fable; and the genre transmits a "moral rule," not a "precept." Nor does an image suffice: a fabulist must construct an action.

An image can indeed illustrate a moral but cannot in itself constitute a fable, which demands plot or action, "a series of changes which together make up a whole" (v, 166). Lessing points to the traditional Aesopian fable which draws a moral from the description of smaller fish escaping from a fisherman's net while the larger, more impressive ones are caught. It presents an image rather than an action, he claims, and thus falls short of being a legitimate fable. Finally, the plot of the fable must constitute a unified whole: "This unity of the fable rests on the agreement of all parts to an ultimate purpose" (v, 166). The ultimate purpose is, of course, the moral lesson.

Attending next to Breitinger's two definitions of the genre, Lessing traces one of them directly to La Motte: "a lesson and instruction disguised under the well-advised allegory of a similar action" (v, 169). Not only is the definition extracted from La Motte's discourse, complains Lessing, but it offers a "diluted" version of the original. He questions whether the adjectives "well-advised" and "similar" contribute to the definition—even what they denote within the context of it. Furthermore, adjectives denoting "disguised" or "hidden," used by La Motte, Richer, and Breitinger, misconstrue the method of the fable. Lessing avers that the fabulist, far from concealing the moral, takes pains to ensure its ultimate revelation: "it must take absolutely no effort to recognize the moral in the fable; on the contrary, if I may say so, it must take effort and constraint not to recognize it" (v, 169). He promptly moderates this vigorous assertion, however, by admitting that the adjective "concealed" might appropriately describe the moral of a complex fable, which is allegorical, but never that of a simple one. Nothing, however, mitigates Lessing's overall scorn of Breitinger's theory of the fable, which he relegates to the same debased level as the utterings of the "beautifully sophistic French" (v, 170). Lessing reserves comment on Breitinger's definition of the fable based on the notion of wonder for the second essay, which discusses the use of animals.

Batteux stands next in the line of fable theorists whom Lessing summons to face his critical judgment. His definition, "the apologue is the account of an allegorical action," receives the same strictures as previous ones in regard to allegory. The specification of "action" conforms better with Lessing's own ideas; but Batteux's assertion that it depends on reason, choice, and purpose comes under sharp attack. Lessing replies that such a definition eliminates nine-tenths of existing fables, and he offers an example from among those excluded: two roosters fight; as the winner crows his victory to the world, a passing eagle notices him, swoops down, and carries him off. Reason and choice have little bearing on the outcome of this episode, proclaims Lessing; the course of events depends primarily on "human" weakness—pride, in this case, which impels the rooster publicly to exult—and partly on the fortuitous presence of the eagle overhead.

Lessing traces Batteux's fundamental error to his confusion of the plot of a fable with the plot of an epic or drama. They are not identical, in Lessing's opinion, nor do the three genre's pursue the same objective. Epic and dramatic plots operate according to reason, choice, and purpose and aspire to arouse passions by portraying them artificially. The fable, on the other hand, avoids touching the emotions of its audience. The fabulist concentrates on the *anschauende Erkenntnis,* the intuitive knowledge, of his readers, by which means he attempts to convince of a single moral truth. Aiming for moral persuasion, he has nothing more to say once this proposal has been carried out and promptly terminates the fable: "he often abandons his characters midway and does not even think about satisfying our curiosity in regard to them" (v, 176). If the fabulist prolongs the narrative after the moral point has been made, he not only adds nothing of value but incurs the danger of obscuring the moral lesson. The plot of the fable frequently seems, therefore, "cut off" rather than ended, a denouement unsatisfactory for epic or drama. It is, however, an approved ending of the fable.

Lessing's *anschauende Erkenntnis* (intuitive knowledge or recognition), a term which he apparently adapted from Christian Wolff, has attracted the attention of critics, one of whom has suggested that Lessing's concept and terminology mark him as a predecessor of Kant.[2]

Although Lessing does not analyze the concept in any of his essays, he uses it as the key to the instructive process of the fable, which, as he describes it, is reminiscent of Marmontel in certain respects. Marmontel, it will be recalled, asserts that the fable warns, thereby activating moral knowledge already existing, at least latently, in the reader. Lessing's "intuitive knowledge" similarly indicates pre-existing moral knowledge. Lessing, however, employs "convince" (*überzeugen*), which designates a function rejected by Marmontel, who considers moral instruction to be continued admonitions in order to maintain the reason alert to its moral responsibility. Marmontel implies that without these warnings man might drift into moral indifference, if not outright immorality. In Lessing's interpretation, on the other hand, each fable aspires to produce a miniature revelation; and indeed he recognizes no fundamental difference between education and revelation. In *Die Erziehung des Menschengeschlechts* (*The Education of the Human Race,* 1780) he elucidates the relationship between them: "Education is revelation which occurs to the individual person; and revelation is education which has occurred to the human race and still occurs" (II, 280). Neither education nor revelation implants anything not inherent in man, but both serve to make the process of realizing innate potential swifter and easier than if the reason were left strictly to its own resources. The fabulist, therefore, appeals to the inherent good sense of the reader; but one could also describe each fable, from Lessing's point of view, as an integral part of a continuing revelation.

With the critical volley fired at Batteux, Lessing ends his barrage at previous definitions and begins to formulate one of his own. He stresses that the fable must affect an air of realism and, to this end, must present a specific case. Man recognizes general moral principles only through the single, specific instance: "The general exists only in the specific and can be intuitively recognized only in the specific" (V, 181). To consider this distinction from another perspective, we may follow Lessing's differentiation of the moral tale from parable to example to fable. A parable depicts a general situation. An example, on the other hand, refers to a specific instance but suggests it as *possible* rather than declaring it *real,* with an "if" or "as if" either stated or implied. The fable treats the specific instance as an actual occurrence, which is the most effective teaching method because the "true case" provides better motivation and can distinguish more clearly than the merely possible. Following here and throughout his discussion a pattern of overstatement and then partial retraction, Lessing initially asserts that truth is recognizable *only* in the single, actual occurrence and then amends his assertion to *more easily* recognizable. He at first implies that the truth of the parable, which speaks in general, remains inscrutable but then modifies the implication to suggest that generalized truth is less readily perceived than particular. Lessing similarly denies allegory in the fable but then reconciles himself to the complex category, which comprises allegorical fables.

Lessing closes the first essay with his own carefully formulated definition of the fable: "When we reduce a general moral principle to a specific case, grant this specific case reality, and invent a story from it in which the general principle is intuitively recognizable, this invention is called a fable" (v, 185).

The other four essays consider various aspects or applications of the fable and thereby supplement the fundamental concepts of the first essay. In the second one Lessing turns to the use of animals and remarks at the outset that previous commentators have avoided or passed over this point. Batteux, for example, declares that the fable traditionally employs animals but then fails to discuss why—a neglect which Lessing curtly dismisses as completely "*à la Françoise!*" (v, 185). Of all fable critics only Breitinger delves into reasons, concluding, as we have seen, that animal and other non-human characters infuse the fable with an attractive sense of wonder. Breitinger defines the fable, moreover, as "an instructive wonder," which is the second of his two definitions noted by Lessing in the first essay.

Lessing, however, challenges the notion that brute characters arouse wonder. Wonder means "to cast off the appearance of truth and possibility" (v, 187), and he doubts that the Ancients had such frivolous intentions when they introduced animals into the fable. They undoubtedly sought, on the contrary, to restrict departures from truth. To this end the fable strives to make the presence of talking, reasoning beasts seem as natural as possible, an impression which the traditional introductory phrase "Once upon a time, when animals still talked . . ." reinforces by giving a historical perspective to the narrative. Lessing concludes that, far from being enthralled by wonder and fantasy, people invariably accept the naturalness of the fable world.

Why then does the fable employ animals? Popular opinion associates certain characteristics and qualities with specific animals. The fabulist takes advantage of this association and selects animals appropriate to his purpose, well aware of the impression that mere introduction of them into the narrative will make on the reader's mind. Human beings, plants, and inanimate things bear with them fewer automatic associations and thus require explanations and descriptions, which draw out and complicate the narrative. In thus referring to the qualities and actions universally accorded animals in order to explain their usefulness, Lessing implies that they are convenient symbols and, in so doing, lodges the fable in the realm of allegory, despite his repeated attempts to establish it elsewhere. If the fabulist employs brute characters because of their symbolic relationships, the plot of the fable therefore involves the interaction of symbolic characters; and it becomes difficult to deny that the fable—even the simple fable—is allegorical.

Lessing also submits a secondary rationale for animal characters. The fabulist avoids touching the emotions of his readers, aiming for moral understanding rather than sensuous involvement. Brute characters help to maintain the reader's emotional detachment since the relationship of man and animal excludes the intimacy that complicates human relationships.

Lessing devotes his third essay to the classification of fables. Going beyond the rudimentary simple and complex categories originally introduced in his first essay, he takes as his starting point the traditional tripartite classification based on the kind of characters employed, which we have seen used by Le Bossu, Batteux, and others and which Lessing himself traces to Aphthonius in the fifth century:

reasonable, which use human character; *moral,* which use dumb beasts; and *mixed,* which use both man and beast (v, 195). But Lessing presents the classification primarily to remark its shortcomings, such as lack of a category to accommodate fables dealing with gods and allegorical figures. To rectify this and other deficiencies he remodels the system, retaining the three categories but redefining them. *Reasonable* now designates those fables "in which the specific case is completely possible" (v, 199). Fables of this category maintain verisimilitude and never present characters, whether animal, inanimate, or human, whose performances exceed their native attributes and capabilities. *Moral* fables, on the other hand, are "possible only after certain presuppositions." The fabulist takes advantage of poetic license to embellish nature, incorporating such unnatural phenomena as talking animals into the narrative. An element of fantasy thus conditions moral fables, but characters must still remain true to their basic dispositions: a tenderhearted wolf or a vicious lamb, for example, would exceed the bounds of credibility. The moral category contains two subcategories: *mythical,* "fables in which the characters are presupposed"; and *hyperphysical,* "in which only *heightened* qualities of real characters are admitted" (v, 200). Gods, ghosts, and other ethereal beings fall into the first subcategory, whereas characters with exaggerated human qualities, such as giants and prophets, compose the second. Finally, the third category, mixed fables, includes, as in previous delineations of the tripartite system, combinations of reasonable and moral.

Lessing emphasizes that his improved system eliminates classification on the relatively unimportant basis of type of characters presented and concentrates on artistic treatment of the characters. If the fabulist restricts them to their native capabilities, the fable belongs to the reasonable category; if he grants additional capabilities to one or more characters or employs supernatural ones, the fable then belongs to one of the other categories.

Lessing's fourth essay concerns form and style, for which he considers Aesop the paragon. Stripped of all unnecessary material and effects, Aesop's fables advance with admirable precision and unerring directness to the moral point. Lessing reminds his readers that the Ancients considered the fable a philosophical instrument, not a poetic genre. Aristotle, he·points out, discusses it under rhetoric. This estimation of the purpose of the fable prevailed until modern times—until La Fontaine, to be exact. The French fabulist removed the fable from philosophy, where its moral purpose was unquestioned and absolute, and transformed it into a poetic genre. "This singular genius! La Fontaine! No, I have nothing against him; but against his imitators, against his blind worshippers!" (v, 208). While appreciating La Fontaine's poetic accomplishments, Lessing regrets the damage rendered the genre by his example: "He succeeded in making a charming poetical toy out of the fable; he fascinated; he got a mass of imitators who thought there was no cheaper way to obtain the name of poet than through enlarged, diluted fables in jolly verse" (v, 210). The unfortunate result of La Fontaine's artistically admirable example has been the degeneration of the fable into "a child's toy."

Seeking to counteract this degeneration, Lessing urges a return to the concise, direct, morally purposeful fable that Aesop produced. Designed to instruct, not entertain, it should be "short and dry," eschewing all extraneous ornamentation. Prose is the appropriate medium for the genre, Lessing declares, since verse invariably leads to discursiveness and resulting diminution of moral force. By revivifying the Aesopian model for fabulists to follow, he hopes to restore the fable to philosophy.

Lessing's final essay discusses a special application of fables in the schools, in addition to the customary use of them as a vehicle for moral instruction. Fables function according to an inductive process by which a truth is drawn from a portrayed event, Lessing points out; and the individual reader unavoidably employs an identical inductive process when he peruses the narrated event and then perceives the moral truth derived from it. The teacher can use the fable to develop his pupils' powers of reasoning by allowing them to discover the moral truth on their own. Lessing recommends making the exercise into an entertaining "hunt." Once the pupils have successfully "bagged the game,'' the teacher can invent other circumstances so that a different moral becomes inducible from the same basic fable. The pupils will eventually be able to invent their own fables. At this point discovery becomes invention: instead of following an inductive process prepared for them, they now engage in original thinking. Lessing explains that the exercise does not aim to make a poet of every child but to develop his inherent powers of invention and discovery.

Despite Lessing's present claim that the fable should be, and originally was, an adjunct of philosophy, for a more balanced judgment it seems best to return to his earlier statement, quoted above, which describes the genre as a blend of poetry and moral. The lament that the fable properly pertains to philosophy and has been perverted by modern versifiers apparently surges up during his heated attack on the imitators of La Fontaine. It overstates his case for a return to the simple, direct fable of Aesop; but Lessing makes a regular use of over-statement in his discussion of the fable, for example, his ultimately untenable denial of anything allegorical in the genre. It seems to be a tactic adopted to demolish opponents. He aims to land a solid blow, fair or foul, to knock out the adversary, rather than to advance by a series of careful, convincing jabs. Lessing apparently could more than hold his own in the rough and tumble literary arguments of the time. Such overstatements-become-misstatements detract from the quality of his essays on the fable, however, despite the overall lucidity of his presentation. Lessing sacrifices balanced argument in order to mount an aggressive campaign for the kind of fable he wants and to demolish critics who hold other views.

Lessing maintains that the fable teaches by stimulating or activating intuitive knowledge. As discussed earlier, L'Estrange and others, echoing Locke, rejected the notion of innate ideas and regarded the mind of the newborn as a blank sheet of paper. Education consisted of filling it with beneficial lessons, with morality foremost, before uncontrolled experience scribbled it beyond social utility and personal integrity. The fable accomplished superbly this pedagogical task because it instructed without pain and because it attracted young, unformed

minds, the critical period for education. Lessing, as well as Marmontel, tends to view man as born with a stock of intuitive knowledge,
including latent moral understanding. Rather than writing on a blank
sheet of paper, the fable jolts this inborn knowledge into active service. The process consists of a personal revelation, according to Lessing; of a reminder, according to Marmontel. In neither case is anything new inscribed in the mind. The trend is from the rational,
materialistic concept of the human mind, and consequently of education, toward the intuitive, inspirational viewpoint. At this point in the
trend the fable still serves its didactic purpose, but at a later stage of
development naked didacticism starts to arouse skepticism. At that
later point the fable meets with less enthusiasm in literary and educational circles.

Lessing's fables and essays had an enormous influence on later
writers in the genre, especially in the German world. Subsequent German critics frequently seem to regard Lessing's fable theory as definitive, dismissing other formulations as either relatively insignificant
forerunners or supplementary commentaries.[3] Although such a view
exaggerates Lessing's role, it is true that his is the only theoretical
work on the fable which has received extensive critical attention in
modern times. Continued interest is undoubtedly due to Lessing's literary-historical stature in general rather than to particular concern for
his ideas on this now mostly ignored genre, but it has been suggested
that he intended his call for restoration of the fable to imply renovation
of all literature.[4]

Also characteristic of subsequent German critics is a division of
the fable, either explicit or tacit, into two broad categories: "Lessingsche" and "Lafontainsche." [5] The former, short and simple,
drives unswervingly to the moral point, while the latter indulges in poetical flourishes. Lessing would perhaps have been flattered to find his
name attached to the fable formula which he advocated, but he himself
would probably have denominated the two categories "Aesopian" and
"degenerate." Although his "back-to-Aesop" campaign was undoubtedly conducted with excellent intentions and with considerable

justification, his notion of reformation tends to exude an air of asceticism, possibly due to polemical excess and thus not wholly intentional. In any case, an ascetic tone pervades his notion of the fable—in his rejection of all poetic trappings, in his apparent condemnation of any playfulness and humor, and in his demand for a stern, direct moral lesson. Many of Lessing's contemporaries praised the critical perceptions in his *Essays* and applauded his effort to "purify" the fable but were also dismayed by the reactionary aspect of his proposed reformation. The fable, it was felt, had assumed a permanent position among the poetic genres.

Melchior Grimm was one of those who responded favorably to Lessing's ideas but at the same time rejected his excessive austerity. In his *Correspondance littéraire* (letter of 1 December 1764) Grimm praises Lessing as fabulist and fable-critic but criticizes him for being "too metaphysical or scholastic." [6] In a subsequent letter he declares that Lessing's own attempts form more of a collection of maxims and witticisms than of fables.[7] A similar but more explicit criticism characterizes a review of Lessing's fables and essays in the periodical *Bibliothek der schönen Wissenschaft und der freyen Kunst*.[8] The reviewer commends the collection but questions, in the first place, whether Lessing's own fables are really so "short and dry" and Aesopian as their author claims. Secondly, he expresses misgivings about Lessing's insistent denial of allegory in the genre. Finally, he is disheartened by Lessing's blanket rejection of all poetical qualities and counters his proposed austerity by claiming that La Fontaine's lyrical fables represent a progressive advancement for the genre rather than a degeneration. Moral instruction appertains to poetry as well as philosophy, the reviewer maintains; and the fable genre is sufficiently capacious to admit two varieties, the short, blunt Aesopian and the charming poetical one.

The most vigorous, thorough, and, in a way, foolish response to Lessing's puritanical crusade came from Johann Jacob Bodmer, who published his *Lessingsche unäsopische Fabeln* (*Lessing's Unaesopian Fables*) in Zurich in 1760, the year after Lessing's *Fabeln: Drei*

Bücher and the accompanying essays. Bodmer launches his rebuttal with attempted parodies of Lessing, whom he derides as the follower of and successor to Daniel Stoppe, the Gottschedian fabulist whose mediocre and sometimes outlandish creations had long been the butt of caustic wit and comment from the Swiss faction. In Fable I Bodmer the parodist explains how he began writing these fables: a faun Capriccio informs him that Stoppe has been replaced as model fabulist by Lessing, who has been "bestowed upon mankind." [9] Capriccio then delivers his version of Lessing's fable theory: "Why does the fable need charm? Would you spice the spices? Short and dry; our teacher demands nothing more; good prose. . . . Excuse your ineptitude with that; make an oracle out of your whims, you will be neither the first nor the last to do so" (pp. 6–7). By means of the parodies Bodmer apparently hoped to laugh Lessing's fables and theory out of serious consideration. In retrospect the attempt appears misguided, for his talent as a parodist was not equal to the task. The equation of the respected and formidable Lessing with the lowly Stoppe, moreover, was an exaggeration which none but the most biased readers could accept.

Bodmer's parodic fables are followed by an extensive refutation of Lessing's theoretical concepts; and it is perhaps regrettable that this "Inquiry into Mr. Lessing's Essays" is associated with the abortive parodies, for it contains much reasoned, valid criticism of his fable theory. Although suffering from lack of organization and occasional dubious conclusions, it remains the most intelligent piece that Bodmer wrote on the genre.

Bodmer takes Lessing to task for his presumptuous, devastating rejection of all previous definitions and for replacing them with one of his own so vague that it covers "all instructive but also sensuous [*sinnlich*] representations." [10] In the process of demolishing his predecessors, moreover, Lessing simplifies the art of fable writing to such an extent that, according to his conception, a half-wit could dash them off using whatever material was at hand. Bodmer contrasts Lessing's and what he deems the accepted definition of the fable: "a general lesson sensuously presented under the allegory of a similar action"

(p. 194). "Action," or "plot," implies *"choice* and *aims* by the persons who undertake an action." Allegory, which is indispensable, serves to join wonder to plausibility, which marks the first time that Bodmer has indicated Breitinger's wonder as a major characteristic of the fable. Finally, he explains that the genre proposes "to present a moral lesson sensuously and vividly." Lessing, Bodmer complains, discards all of these fundamental components and in essence forsakes the fable, substituting what amounts to little more than a glorified epigram. The Lessing formula results in a dull, dry narration brightened only by the magic formula "Once upon a time." It prescribes a new form, or at least a novel variation, which has no affinity to the fable as Aesop wrote it, despite Lessing's assertions to the contrary.

Bodmer's further accusation that Lessing attempts to do away with plot in the fable seems a misinterpretation of the latter's argument: Lessing's substitution of "a specific instance" for "plot" or "action" amounts largely to a matter of semantics. Bodmer insists, however, that elimination of plot would nullify all difference between the fable and the parable, the example, and other kindred forms. Contending that allegory is an inescapable complement to comparison, he sensibly declares that the fable, by definition, compares the actions of its characters with typical human actions and, therefore, inescapably revolves on allegory. Bodmer notes Lessing's admission that it exists in complex fables; and he asserts that all fables are constructed on the same principle, no matter what Lessing chooses to call it.

Bodmer cites both Socrates and Breitinger to buttress his opinion that, the fable being poetry, an element of wonder is essential. Only human ones dispense with it. But such realistic depictions cannot be considered poetry and are more accurately classified as examples or parables rather than fables. Poetic expression, invention, and adornment differentiate the fable from the straightforward example; and these agreeable attributes also strengthen its effectiveness as a means of moral instruction. And to perorate his argument, Bodmer defines the fable as "a fictitious example" (p. 302).

Bodmer contends with Lessing on a variety of other points, as one might expect, since at 160 pages his rebuttal is considerably longer than the five *Essays*. Occasionally his argument descends to the level of quibbling; and at other times his point of dissension remains ambiguous—for example, his objections to Lessing's remodeled system of classification. Interesting, however, is his retort to Lessing's contention that the fable cannot be extended to the length of the epic and still remain a fable. Bodmer refers to Mandeville's *The Fable of the Bees* as a possible example of an "Aesopian epic," noting that the work seems a typical, allegory-based Aesopian fable, which has been drawn to epic length without losing the unity and force of its original moral point. Intriguing as the idea might be, it would seem to contradict Bodmer's own contention, expressed in his earlier discussions of the genre, that the animal fable must remain short and uncomplicated due to the inherent limitations of animals in human roles.

Lessing, of course, did not fail to notice Bodmer's attack on him; and he astutely seized on the attempted parodies as a convenient focus for an inevitable reply, in which he affects to identify the parodist with the fable writer and critic Hermann Axel whom Bodmer had invented to ridicule the Gottschedian fabulists.[11] Lessing's riposte adds nothing to his own fable theory, nor does it subtract anything from Bodmer's. It mainly serves to demonstrate Lessing's skill as a literary brawler, capable of returning blow for blow and insult for insult. Bodmer's criticism of Lessing's fables and theory drew support, however, from a rather unexpected source. An article in *Das Neueste aus der anmuthigen Gelehrsamkeit,* a Gottschedian periodical, champions the faction's traditional enemy Bodmer over Lessing, whom it compares to a pampered child, so spoiled by acclaim and attention that he considers himself authorized to expound oracularly on any literary matter. The article applauds Bodmer's firm rebuttal and reprints several pages from his *Lessingsche unäsophische Fabeln.*[12]

Although fiercely critical of Lessing in this work, Bodmer unmistakably admires the fable itself. Nine years later, however, his attitude toward the genre shows a significant change. In the preface to *Historische Erzählungen* (*Historical Tales,* 1769) he rejects fables and other invented stories in favor of those based on historical reality: "Historical events indeed have a great advantage over invented ones; there is more certainty with them that they describe correctly according to nature and lie less. For this reason they are far preferable to fables, even Aesopian ones." [13] Fables are suitable to entertain and instruct adults, who have experience and knowledge of the world; but for children they are mostly incomprehensible and frequently dangerous, since they "draw a cover over the truth." Using La Fontaine as an example, Bodmer discovers in his fables "a thousand features and instructions . . . which are far beyond the experiences and capabilities of children." He points out that children invariably find the naked, unadorned truth hard enough to discover and understand.

Bodmer's scepticism about the fable, even his reference to La Fontaine in order to illustrate its difficulties and ambiguities for children, suggests that by this time he had read Rousseau's criticism of the genre in *Émile*. The ideas of Rousseau and others on the role of the fable in pedagogy call for a new chapter.

CHAPTER EIGHT

Rousseau and the Fable in Education

The first chapter of this study sketches the role of the fable in the pedagogical ideas of Locke and Fénelon, both of them progressive educators who condemn "strong-arm" teaching methods. They recommend the fable as a painless means of leading children to morality and learning. Offer a child a story and his interest is immediately aroused, after which the motivation derives from within, requiring no more than gentle guidance by the teacher. The foregoing chapter notes that Lessing extends the possible classroom application of fables beyond their customary employment to instill moral virtue, showing how teachers can utilize them to develop original thinking in their students.

Fables, however, were an established item in the classroom curriculum well before Locke, Fénelon, and other progressive educators. Aesop had long been indispensable to children's literature, and pupils typically left the grammar schools with Phaedrus' Latin versions stuffed grammatically and syntactically into their heads. Sir Roger L'Estrange condemns this mechanical learning and reciting in the preface to his collection and aims to provide a comprehensible English version of traditional fables.[1] Memorization, whether in Latin or in the vernacular, was a normal requirement. Edmund Arwaker, for example, recommends his 1708 collection by asserting that his use of verse will assist in engraving the fables on the memory.[2] Henri Richer also assumes rote learning and considers it sufficient reason for avoiding excessive length.

Although fabulists typically declare allegiance to the ideal of brevity, it is common to find their creations drawn out by extensive sermons to ensure that the reader, child or adult, will extract every grain of moral nutrition. L'Estrange's volume illustrates this lengthy sermonizing; and supplementing his own copious exegeses are the *Remarks* on his fables, purportedly by James Gordon, Bishop of Aberdeen,[3] which elucidate further moral lessons and supply additional historical and literary applications. In the preface to a two-volume collection *Les Fables d'Esope Phrigien* (1709), which went through several editions, the Abbé Bellegarde stresses his overriding didactic purpose: "In order to extract all possible fruit from Aesop's fables, one cannot stop simply at the letter; it is necessary to penetrate into the spirit of the fable, where one can imbibe of beautiful lessons." [4] The abbé attaches a detailed *sens moral* to each of his fables; and the preface to a German version of his collection advertises imaginative expansion of these already protracted morals: "The moral lessons have been greatly extended, in a hundred different ways altered and multiplied, in order that everyone can find one among them suited to his situation and to the capabilities of his intellect." [5] In both the French original and the German translation an easily-memorized quatrain, summarizing the moral lesson, concludes each fable.

Three works by Johann Georg Sulzer provide an insight into the pedagogical use of fables. A native Swiss, Sulzer was an educator and man of letters trained in Bodmer's school of influence who later migrated to Berlin. His encyclopedic *Allgemeine Theorie der schönen Künste* (*General Theory of the Fine Arts*) relates to the discussion in Chapter x. The pedagogical treatises have a bearing on matters at this point.

In *Versuch von der Erziehung und Unterweisung der Kinder* (*Experiment in the Education and Instruction of Children,* 1748) Sulzer delineates two methods to teach people: by means of precepts and by means of examples.[6] The first, which avoids circuitous narration in favor of didactic directness, is normally adopted by preachers. The second follows a more devious approach through the senses but by so

doing effects a firmer implantation of the lesson. Concluding, therefore, that instruction by example is usually preferable, Sulzer lists
three kinds: 1) the "living" example taken from the surroundings; 2)
histories, which can be either "true histories or invented stories"
(p. 111); and 3) the Aesopian fable, which has the advantage of teaching even more indirectly than the others. Sulzer favors the latter,
especially for older children, but warns that many fables present bad
examples, necessitating careful selection of those in which "the virtues shine forth more strongly than the weaknesses. . . . Of such
fables one must have a special collection only for children and read or
tell them so often that the children learn them by memory, in order
that they can remember them on their own when the opportunity
arises" (p. 114). Rote learning, once again, is the ultimate aim, based
on the notion that the composite of memorized fables will serve the
child—and indeed the adult—as a guidebook to proper conduct in
daily life.

Sulzer advises the teacher first to acquaint young children with
simple *Märchen* and to reserve fables until maturity enables them to
understand and benefit from the moral lesson. He particularly recommends the fables of Fénelon and of Meyer von Knonau. Although
prescribing memorization, Sulzer does advocate treating older children
less mechanically and according them the opportunity to think for
themselves. With maturity, moreover, religious training should comprise an increasing portion of their lessons. Sulzer seems to sanction
Fénelon's pattern of education, at least in its broad outlines: fables
constitute the intermediate stage of a process that begins with innocent
tales and culminates with religious instruction.

Sulzer's *Vorübungen zur Erweckung der Aufmerksamkeit und des
Nachdenkens* (*Preparatory Exercises to the Awakening of Alertness
and Reflection,* 1768) outlines a graduated pattern of instruction ex-
tending from the lower grades through the gymnasium. Fables of
various degrees of sophistication contribute to the material for each
level. Sulzer declares that teachers invariably meet with better results
in instructing children when they have recourse to animals, especially

exotic ones such as the lion. Animals immediately arouse juvenile attentions so that lessons may be inculcated without resort to pressure. For most effective use of a fable, Sulzer counsels the teacher to begin by reading it orally several times and then to call upon pupils to recite it until each can do it without faltering. The student commits the fable to memory in order to have the moral guidance perpetually at hand, while the repeated recitation also provides practice in eloquence and rhetoric. Once all have recited and have demonstrated successful memorization, the teacher should undertake an informal discourse to elucidate the moral and the reasoning of the characters involved and ultimately to relate the lesson to the pupils' own lives. One thing leading to another, the teacher can illuminate multiple ramifications and applications of the fable, all depending on the time available.

In apparent contrast to educators of Sulzer's ilk, Jean-Jacques Rousseau denounces the practice of subjecting young children to fables, an opinion most completely formulated in his pedagogical novel *Émile*. The contrast, however, is more appearance than reality. Far from condemning the genre, Rousseau recognizes its instructive value. He objects primarily to La Fontaine's sophisticated, poetical fables as material for young children and to the common practice of forcing memorization and recitation of them. Rousseau, like Locke, deplores the constant memorization demanded of children; part of his criticism aims, therefore, not at fables themselves but at their customary employment as material for memorization. Young children learn and recite them but do not understand them. Rousseau does approve fables, on the other hand, for youths sufficiently mature to comprehend them and to profit from the moral lesson.

The novel *Julie* (1761) contains a preliminary sketch of the fuller criticism to come. Discussing her method of educating her children, Julie tells of her attempt to relate one of La Fontaine's fables to her oldest son, with the intention of both amusing him and arousing his interest in reading. She had no more than commenced before he asked her if ravens and foxes and other animals could indeed talk. Julie confesses her dismay upon recognizing the impossibility of differentiating for her son between a fable and a falsehood. She laid aside La Fontaine, convinced that fables are suitable for grown men but that the plain truth must be told to children.[7]

Émile (1762) discusses in more detail the difficulties that Julie had experienced.[8] According to Rousseau, reading fables, for a child, may be identical to undertaking a volume of history or philosophy: he sees only words printed lineally on a page. Or, he may hear and be charmed by the story, find the moral tag amusing, but completely miss the underlying truth. Rousseau claims that children between five and twelve are incapable of understanding abstractions. They grasp what lies within the range of their own senses and experience but remain puzzled by anything that requires abstract reasoning. When children undertake fables, both the incredible world of talking animals and the indirect manner of approaching truth surpass their capabilities: "All children are made to learn La Fontaine's fables, and there is not a single one who undertands them." [9] It is just as well, moreover, that they do not, for the morality of fables contains so many complications and typically consorts with such an admixture of immorality that it would be just as likely to inspire them to vice as to virtue. Poetry, although facilitating memorization, further hinders comprehension, as does any kind of artistic language and syntax. These multiple complications, Rousseau contends, result in cute but mindless recitations by little children who have no understanding of the words they spout.

Rousseau remarks the existence of fables written especially for children but neither designates them nor defines the qualities governing their acceptability—nor does he state whether *he* would approve them. He finds among La Fontaine's fables, however, only five or six clearly endowed with "juvenile naiveté" (IV, 352). But he demonstrates the insurmountable difficulties of even the most simple and appropriate, "The Fox and the Crow," in which the former, by means of flattery, tricks the latter into dropping the cheese so that he can devour it himself. Rousseau selects this fable as La Fontaine's masterpiece if his aim were really to be understood by children and to please and instruct them. It awakens, nevertheless, a multitude of questions in young minds: what is a crow? how can he hold a cheese in his beak? do foxes and crows really talk? Many of the questions arise naturally from childish curiosity, but others derive from conflicts with nature inherent to the fable. Still others stem from the poetic language. Narration of the fable becomes entangled and ultimately lost in the explanations necessary to make it intelligible. The child will, in any case, never understand lines of subtlety and mockery, no matter how carefully they are explained.

One might argue that lack of understanding merely results in a neutral effect and that if the child learns something from his continual questioning he still profits from hearing the fable. Rousseau warns, however, of possible adverse influence: should a six-year-old child be introduced to people who flatter and lie for the sake of gain? One faces the considerable danger of teaching the child how to beguile another into dropping his cheese rather than of admonishing him to hold on to his own: "Watch children learning their fables, and you will see that when they are at the point of applying them they almost always do it contrary to the author's intention; instead of observing the fault from which he wants to cure or save them, they tend to love the vice with which one takes advantage of the faults of others. In the foregoing fable children make fun of the crow, but they all feel affection for the fox" (IV, 356). Guided by self-love, children invariably associate with the principal role in any story or drama. A fox is "cute" and smart. Children side with him no matter what skulduggery he engages in, just as they inevitably associate with a lion, one of the animals most attractive to them. As a result, claims Rousseau, they frequently learn vice rather than virtue from the fable. Even while accepting the validity of his claim, one might wonder whether the outcome would differ markedly with adults, who could be even more prone to associate with the quick-thinking, aggressive animals.

Book III of *Émile* covers the child's education from age twelve to fifteen, and Book IV, after fifteen, which Rousseau denominates the social stage of education. This age, which marks the maturing youth's entrance into the world and his initial experiences of its ways, is the time for fables. Now he can understand the fox's cunning flattery of the crow because he has been a victim of flattery himself. The fable engraves in his mind the harsh experience, ensuring that he will remember it and thereby profit from having undergone it. Stressing the need for vivid impression, Rousseau denounces the common practice of appending an explicit moral tag: the reader should be required to discover the moral for himself—a dictum which fits into Rousseau's overall policy of learning by experience. If the reader cannot comprehend the fable without the explanatory tag, he will not fathom it with the tag either. Such explicitness, moreover, restricts the possible applications of the fable, which might sprout multiple edifying ramifications if the reader is left to his own imagination. Rousseau concludes that, in any case, only an experienced person can grasp the moral and perceive applications of it.

Rousseau, therefore, welcomes the fable as an effective means of defining and stressing the lessons of experience. He rejects the genre for young children lacking acquaintance with the world and thus incapable of understanding the lessons; but when all is said and done, his warning about its limitations for children and his method of utilizing fables for youths does not materially differ from Sulzer's program. Sulzer, an avowed advocate of fables, advises the teacher to select carefully the ones that present exclusively virtuous examples, to reserve them for older, experienced children able to discern the moral, and to apply the lessons to the personal experiences of his pupils. Sulzer approaches fables positively, whereas Rousseau focuses on possible detrimental results; but the latter's negative approach merely warns of practical limitations and should not be construed as a condemnation of the genre. Despite his adverse criticism, Rousseau still recognizes the educational value of fables.

Other critics and educators also express reservations about using the genre to instruct children. In *Introduction to the Art of Thinking* (1761), an anthology of short edifying pieces, Lord Kames includes fables, among which are a few of La Motte's in French; but he confesses mixed feelings about admitting them to the volume: "To disguise men under the mask of goats and bulls, leads to little other purpose than to obscure the moral instruction. Stories, real or invented, where persons are introduced in their native appearance, serve much better for illustration." [10]

Melchior Grimm, in his *Correspondance littéraire* (letter of 15 October 1762), agrees with Rousseau that La Fontaine's sophisticated fables should not be given to children: "the genius of La Fontaine is so full of subtleties and original twists that it is impossible for children to understand it, and even more to sense its merit." [11] But these difficulties, he explains, do not apply to the creations of Aesop and Phaedrus, whose "narration is as simple as their moral aim." Grimm's stricture thus includes only the subtle, poetic fables of La Fontaine, whom he characterizes as perhaps the most difficult of all French poets. Nor is Grimm the only critic who remarks the particular difficulty of this one fabulist. A French version of Aesop, for example, which was dignified by several editions in the course of the eighteenth century, specifies that it contains fables expressly for children, who find La Fontaine's unintelligible. This *Nouveau Recueil des fables d'Esope* (1731) is in prose, for easier reading, but includes a quatrain at the beginning and end of each piece intended for memorization by young readers.

The Abbé Jean-Louis Aubert, whose ideas are discussed in Chapter VI, freely concurs that many of La Fontaine's fables exceed the capabilities of children but scoffs at critics who censure sophisticated fable writing per se. La Fontaine created first-rate *poetry,* he declares; and no one should expect children to understand and appreciate poetry of any genre.[12] Aubert also composed a "Discourse on the Way to Read Fables, or to Recite Them" in which he refutes Rousseau's contentions of futility and possible adverse results in assigning fables to children. Aubert admits frequent failures in comprehension and difficulties in pronunciation but still affirms the value of requiring children to learn and recite them. Aside from exercising their memories, children learn "good sense and intelligence," even if the subtleties and nuances escape their comprehension.[13] To start, one should allow

them to disregard the meter, reciting the verses as simply and prosai-
cally as necessary, and merely ask that they follow the sense of the
narrative. Even if they lose track of the total meaning of the fable, one
can at least expect them to understand isolated phrases and to articu-
late the individual words correctly. The simplified reading or recitation
and the limited understanding represent a valuable beginning, and
complete comprehension will follow.

Christian Gotthilf Salzmann reiterates Rousseau's warning about
the neutral or adverse effect of fables in *Über die wirksamsten Mittel
Kindern Religion beyzubringen* (*On the Most Effective Means of Teaching Children Religion,* 1780), a work in which he, like Fénelon, discusses means of motivating children toward the Bible. Salzmann concludes that stories offer the most fruitful means of achieving this goal
but rejects Biblical stories as introductory material. They concern distant lands, foreign to the child's limited world, and strange, adult people who perplex rather than attract. Fables, declares Salzmann, are
even less suitable, especially those employing animals: "Either the
child believes that animals think and act like men, or he does not
believe it. In the first case he hovers over one of the crudest mistakes.
If he does not believe this, however, if he knows that the entire story
is an invention, the appended moral will lose its credibility as a consequence." [14] At this point Salzmann records his wholehearted agreement with Rousseau and recommends "the stories of good children,"
which avoid both the dangerous fantasies of the fable and the enigmas
of the adult world.

Despite the strictures of Rousseau and others, the publication of
fables did not diminish. There seems to have been, on the contrary, a
continual increase throughout the eighteenth century and into the nineteenth of volumes designed specifically to facilitate the instruction of
children, both in school and at home. François Desbillon's *Fabulae
Aesopiae* (1768), for example, combines instruction in morality and
Latin grammar; and neither the method nor the text differ markedly
from what schoolboys a hundred years earlier were subjected to. Ga-
briello Faerno's Latin versions of traditional fables continued to see

repeated publication in all western European countries. A London edition, *Cent Fables, en Latin et en François* (1744), enables students simultaneously to study both Latin and French. Other bilingual and trilingual editions appeared regularly—and at least one quadrilingual collection, printed in Vienna in the 1820's: *Die Fabeln des Äsopus; Fables d'Esope; Favole di Esopo; Fabulae Aesopi.*

The German world of the latter part of the century shows a particular fondness for instructing children by means of fables. The unwieldy title to one of numerous collections advertises the virtues of the volume: *Esopi Leben und auserlesene Fabeln mit deutlichen Erklärungen, nützlichen Tugendlehren, und hierzu dienlichen saubern Kupfern* (*Aesop's Life and Selected Fables, With Clear Explanations, Useful Moral Lessons, and Pretty Engravings Useful for this Purpose,* 1777). The preface laments the tendency of many existing collections to go over the heads of young people and emphasizes the aim of the present compilation to attract and instruct youths, children, and even pre-readers, whom the engravings will beguile and thereby motivate to learn to read. Reflecting the influence of progressive educators, the editor affirms that education should take the form of a game, although the sermonizing of the text tends to belie this happy intention. Each fable is accompanied by the inevitable exegesis, a lengthy moral lesson, and finally a *Spruch,* consisting of two or four lines of memorizable verse which recapitulate the lesson. The editor of a similar volume containing fables and other moral stories, *Lesebuch für Kinder von 8. 9. bis 10. Jahren* (*Reader for Children from 8–10 Years Old,* 1778), dedicates the collection to both children and parents, informing the latter in glowing terms of the assistance these stories can render in the moral development of their offspring: "With this purpose in mind I gathered together the present fables for parents and children. If the former are serious, love will give them eloquence, and they will find opportunity and words to discuss each fable often and in many ways; and the children will stand about and ask, and let themselves be told, and take each syllable thankfully to heart." [15]

The two foregoing volumes were designed for home use, but

fables also remained prominent in the school curriculum. Johann Ernesti compiled two volumes of literary selections, one intended for the elementary classes of the gymnasium, the other for the advanced: *Praktische Unterweisung in den schönen Wissenschaften für die kleine Jugend* (*Practical Instruction in the Belles-Lettres for Small Youths,* 1778) and *Moralisch praktisches Lehrbuch der schönen Wissenschaften für Jünglinge* (*Moral-Practical Reader in the Belles-Lettres for Youths,* 1779). Both provide moral instruction, introduce the students to literature, and exhibit stylistic models to guide their own attempts at writing. Selections, all short, include Gellert, Lessing, Lichtwer, and other German fabulists, plus distinguished non-Germans such as Aesop and La Fontaine. Johann Friedrich Seidel's *Zweckmässige Fabeln und Erzählungen für die Jugend, zur Deklamationsübung in öffentlichen und Privat-Lehranstalten* (*Useful Fables and Stories for Youths, for Practice in Declamation in Public and Private Educational Institutions,* 1805) proposes all the traditional pedagogical applications of the fable: "In addition to the practice in memorization and declamation, it must not be forgotten to sharpen the power of judgment and to feed and ennoble the feel for morality, right, and virtue." [16]

The genre also merited respectful treatment in such literary textbooks as Johann Jakob Engel's *Anfangsgründe einer Theorie der Dichtungsarten, aus deutschen Mustern entwickelt* (*Rudiments of a Theory of Poetic Styles, Developed from German Examples,* 1780). Engel, professor at the Joachimsthaler Gymnasium in Berlin, envisions his work as an introductory text to literary theory for his more advanced students. Basing the chapter dedicated to the fable on ideas borrowed from Lessing, he explains the non-human characters as an attempt to avoid the emotional involvement consequent to human actions, presents simple and complex categories, and prescribes termination of the fable, even if abrupt, immediately after delivery of the moral. Engel illustrates these theoretical explanations with numerous examples, many of them also drawn from Lessing.

For his textbook *Entwurf einer Theorie und Literatur der schönen Wissenschaften* (*Outline of a Theory and Literature of the Belles-Let-*

tres, 1783), Johann Joachim Eschenburg also derives a chapter on the fable from Lessing. His definition is a virtual restatement of his mentor's. Despite obvious admiration for Lessing, however, Eschenburg eschews his predecessor's asceticism and recognizes "the newer, poetical style of the Aesopian fable," the style of La Fontaine, which Lessing sternly rejected.[17] Eschenburg admits that poetic beautification is not strictly necessary but maintains its legitimacy as an agreeable aspect of the genre. He cites Marmontel in this regard and also agrees with the French critic's delineation of naiveté as the essential quality of a successful fabulist.

Rousseau's criticism of the pedagogical use of fables, as discussed above, thus seems to have had little effect on the publication of volumes for children in the short run. Educators and men of letters continued to recommend them for youngsters of all ages, although perhaps warning that care must be exercised in their selection. In the long run Rousseau's general educational methods, his call for teaching by means of experience, caused far greater damage to the fable's traditional utility. The fable serves best a pedagogy based on didacticism and memorization. When the method shifts so that the teacher tries to stimulate the student to learn by personal experience, the fable's utility diminishes. By criticizing its traditional function as a mnemonic device and by eliminating the moral tag, Rousseau starts it on its way to pedagogical obscurity. He is really demanding something which is not the fable. Innovative educators following in his footsteps, particularly in the nineteenth century, regard the genre with nowhere near the enthusiasm of their predecessors.

CHAPTER NINE

Dodsley and England at Mid-Century

Even though the fable never gained the prestige nor drew the critical attention in England that it did on the continent, it was sufficiently esteemed to attract the talents of a man of literary stature like novelist Samuel Richardson, who published his *Aesop's Fables* in 1740. The subtitle boasts the aim "to promote Religion, Morality, and Universal Benevolence." Richardson declares in the preface that it is his intention to "convince every one concerned in the Business of Education, how careful we have been to collect only such Fables as were fit for the Instruction of the Youth of both Sexes, at the same that we hope it will not be found unworthy of the Perusal of Persons of riper Years and Understanding." [1] Testifying to Richardson's success, as well as to the widespread popularity of the fable, his collection went through several editions and was translated into German by no less a personage than Lessing. [2]

Robert Dodsley, a contemporary of Richardson's, was dramatist, critic, bookseller, publisher for Samuel Johnson, and close friend of Alexander Pope. In 1761 Dodsley published his anthology *Selected Fables of Esop, and other Fabulists,* prefaced by his own "An Essay on Fable" and a life of Aesop. The collection consists of three sections, the first containing fables by the Ancients, the second, by Moderns, and the third, original compositions by Dodsley and his friends—"gentlemen of the most distinguished abilities." [3] "A New Life of Aesop," written by "a learned friend," discards the popular tradition depicting the Greek fabulist as deformed and ugly and portrays him as probably "of a handsome countenance and shape" and perhaps "as full of wit and humour as our celebrated Dr. Swift." [4] It further concedes that Aesop probably did not invent the fable—a not uncommon admission—and ascribes his accreditation with the honor to his unsurpassed excellence in the genre.

Dodsley's "An Essay on Fable" represents the first and only attempt at a thorough study of the genre in England. Although sometimes original, occasionally to the point of quaintness, Dodsley's basic ideas reflect La Motte, whom he acknowledges as his source. [5] And insofar as he relies on La Motte's "Discourse" and ignores an intervening half-century of critical works produced on the Continent, a tinge of anachronism shades Dodsley's discussion. Contemporary with his essay, Hamann, Herder, and others were developing a concept of the genre far removed from La Motte's dependence on classical rules and tradition.

In the introductory segment of his essay, Dodsley, referring to "fable" in the sense of imaginative literary plot, specifies that every one, "whether of the sublimer and more complex kind, as the epic and dramatic; or of the lower and more simple, as what has been called the Esopean, should make it his principal intention to illustrate some one moral or prudential maxim." [6] All literary genres, the prestigious epic as well as the humble Aesopian fable, are identical in their underlying moral purpose; and Dodsley admits that the latter acquires its right to esteem only through its relation to the greater genres. Nevertheless, "a perfect Fable, even of this inferior kind, seems a much stronger proof of genius than the mere narrative of an event" (p. xxxvi). Simple narrative requires only judgment, whereas the creation of a fable, of whatever kind, demands imagination as well.

In the subsequent section of the essay entitled "Of the Truth or Moral of a Fable," Dodsley focuses the discussion exclusively on the *Aesopian* fable and describes it in terms by now familiar: "The very essence of a Fable is to convey some moral or *useful* Truth beneath the shadow of an *allegory*" (p. xxxvii). The assertion faithfully reflects La

Motte, as does the admonition that the truth should be nothing too "obvious, trivial or trite." Dodsley proceeds to list the usually delineated advantages of the fable, such as its "polite manner," which suppresses even the slightest hint of superiority, and the accompanying entertainment, which obviates the resentment that typically hampers instruction.

The fabulist, adjures Dodsley, should, "strictly speaking," avoid "any *detached* or *explicit* Moral," which would expose the didacticism from under the camouflage of amusement and thereby destroy the allegory on which depends the fable's success. Dodsley himself, however, not only attaches moral tags but indexes the morals to the fables in his volume, "in order to give all necessary assistance to young readers" (p. xxxviii). He apologizes for the appended tags by explaining that the greatest fault in any composition is obscurity: it is better "to show *enough* for the less acute, even at the hazard of showing *too much* for the more sagacious" (p. xxxix). If the fabulist decides to attach a moral, it should introduce the fable, declares Dodsley, since a concluding moral tag insults the reader, implying his inability to discover the truth on his own. At the beginning, however, it sets the reader on the right track without giving offense: "He knows the game which he pursues; and, like a beagle on a warm scent, he follows the sport with alacrity, in proportion to his intelligence." Without the prefaced moral, warns Dodsley, the reader remains puzzled throughout and requires a "fresh perusal" of the fable in order to discern it on his own. We are left with the conclusion, therefore, that the fable *does* demand an attached moral tag, despite Dodsley's "strictly speaking" at the outset of his discussion.

The "action, or allegory," must be clear, "one and entire," and natural—"that is, founded, if not on Truth, at least on Probability; on popular opinion" (p. xl). Naturalness requires, for example, that a sheep should not be depicted as the hunting companion of a lion, nor should a lion fall in love with a maiden—a situation frequently criticized for unnaturalness [7]—nor should a fox long for grapes; "and he that should make his Goose lay golden eggs would show a luxuriant *fancy,* but very little *judgment.* In short, nothing beside the faculty of speech and reason, which Fable has been allowed to confer, even upon inanimates, must ever *contradict* the nature of things, or at least the commonly received opinions concerning them" (p. xlii). But accepted tradition permits such fantasies as sirens, goblins, fairies, the sphynx, the phoenix, and the man in the moon: "Here the notoriety of opinion supplies the place of fact, and in this manner truth may fairly be deduced from falsehood."

Dodsley, like others, asserts the preeminence of animal characters. They are more nearly related to man than any other segment of creation, lacking only the power of speech, and retain the simplicity that man has lost. The fabulist, however, is not limited to animals and may employ whatever characters he considers appropriate, a freedom which constitutes his "one advantage over all other writers whatsoever" and which opens an unlimited range "of novelty and variety" (p. xliv). This imaginative carte blanche also makes the fabulist a creator, the first and primary qualification of a poet; but Dodsley once again reminds his readers that the fabulist does not pretend to the distinguished level of epic and tragic poets.

In specifying a familiar but elegant style, the "genteel familiar," Dodsley again borrows from La Motte. La Fontaine's unexcelled fables provide the best stylistic examples, he asserts, and L'Estrange's the worst—familiar, but also "coarse and vulgar" (p. xlvii). Pointing to this bad example, Dodsley declares indispensable a touch of polish to superimpose the *"effect* of art" on the *"appearance* of nature."

Dodsley offers no new insights into the fable and for the most part provides his readers with a delayed echo of La Motte. He begins and ends his essay in an apologetic tone, reflecting the relative insignificance of the fable in English literary circles. His Continental colleagues speak loud and clear, with no fear of being ridiculed for talking seriously about the little fable. Despite Dodsley's apologetic tone and his lack of fresh insights and profundity, his essay and fables attracted a modest but respectful attention. The uniqueness in England of his attempt at a thorough analysis of the genre would in part account for it.

Contemporary reviewers accorded Dodsley's essay and fables

considerable praise. The *Monthly Review,* for example, devotes several pages to an admiring summary of his theoretical principles and characterizes his book as "a very ingenious, a very elegant, and what is of still greater importance, a very useful work . . . a classical performance, both in regard to the elegant simplicity of the stile, and the propriety of sentiments and characters." [8] Robert Anderson, discussing Dodsley in *The Works of the English Poets* (1795), considers his essay "one of the first pieces of criticism, in which rules are delivered for this species of composition drawn from nature, and by which these small and pleasing kind of productions that were thought to have little other standard than the fancy, are brought under the jurisdiction of the judgment. Dodsley has been so eminently successful in his design, that the propriety of his remarks cannot be disputed, except only in one instance." [9] That one instance is Dodsley's objection to the unnaturalness of a fox eating grapes. Anderson reports the observation of a certain Dr. Hasselquist, who comments in his *Travels* that Palestinian grape growers regard the fox a major nuisance because of his nocturnal plundering of their vineyards. The fable of the fox and the grapes rests, therefore, on an empirical foundation, nullifying Dodsley's objection to it. In spite of Dodsley's error in animal gastronomy, however, Anderson optimistically predicts that "his *Essay on Fable* will be a durable monument of his ingenuity" (xi, 81).

The Art of Poetry on a New Plan (1762), printed by John Newbery and revised for him by Oliver Goldsmith, presents young people with an introduction to belles-lettres. In France or Germany of this epoch, a literary work aspiring to attract a youthful audience probably would begin with the fable; but this English text accords it only a brief section buried deep in the first volume, in which sample fables from John Gay, Edward Moore, and others follow a brief introductory commentary. The commentator provides a rather indifferent definition and analysis of the genre: "The Fable differs little from the Tale, except in this, that it is allegorical, and generally introduces animals, and things inanimate, as persons discoursing together, and delivering Precepts for the improvement of Mankind. . . . [It was] invented, we may suppose, to convey truth in an indirect manner. . . . It is always expected that these compositions should inculcate some moral, or useful lesson, for when deficient in this respect, they are of little, or no value." [10] Subsequent sections of the same work equate fable with allegory, narrative and classical mythology.

Oliver Goldsmith has been credited with authorship of "An Essay on Fable" printed in *Bewick's Select Fables* (1784). [11] The essay is cursory, evidently a hack-work introductory piece solicited by the publisher, and does not approach in quality or completeness Dodsley's essay of the same title. The author, whether Goldsmith or another, avails himself of the definition which, by this time, has become a commonplace: "Fable is the method of conveying Truth under the form of an allegory." [12] Its underlying meaning transcends the superficial action, yet this inner truth must be "visible and manifest." In order smoothly to carry out this aim, the action, which constitutes the chief component of the fable, must be single, clear, unified, and probable. Like most critics, the present one declares that "the incidents of a Fable ought to have a real foundation in nature" (p. xxxviii) and that the appetites and passions of non-human characters should harmonize with their native attributes. In apparent reference to Dodsley, he expressly approves the credibility of a grape-eating fox, citing the evidence from Dr. Hasselquist's *Travels* noted above. After scattered comments on various aspects, such as fable style—simple and conversational—he terminates his essay, quite possibly having extracted the totality of his critical perceptions, not to mention the title, from Dodsley.

James Beattie includes an essay "On Fable and Romance" in his *Dissertations Moral and Critical,* but the Aesopian is treated as only one kind of fable and far from the most important. Beattie offhandedly refers to "these little allegories" [13] and takes pains only to emphasize that nature should be no further violated than in granting plants and animals the powers of speech and reason. His examples are interesting: "a fox might play with a tragedian's headpiece; a lamb and a wolf might drink of the same brook, and the former lose his life on the occasion: but who ever heard of an elephant reading Greek, or a hare riding on the back of a calf?'' (p. 507). After these comments on naturalness, Beattie almost immediately moves on to ''the higher sorts of fable,'' which ''please by a more exquisite invention, and a higher probability.'' Concisely describing the other varieties of fable, he eventually arrives at the ''modern romance,'' his primary concern in this essay.

None of the English works discussed above regards the fable as a full-fledged literary genre. Even Dodsley admits its inferiority to the greater genres and traces its modest literary standing entirely to its relationship with epic and drama. It might also be adduced that Lord Kames disdains treatment of the fable in his *Elements of Criticism* (1761). Since he included it, albeit with reservations, in his anthology *Introduction to the Art of Thinking,* mentioned in the foregoing chapter, it would seem that he considered the fable an educational tool but not a legitimate literary genre.

Although the English fabulists and critics discussed here have conceded the fable ambiguous literary merit, they have regarded it as a serious and useful means of moral instruction. Numerous other English fable writers, however, did not grant it such respect. *Fables and Tales for the Ladies* (1750), for example, illustrate only a mild morality of a social and worldly kind. John Hall Stevenson's *Fables for Grown Gentlemen* (1761), which popular demand carried through several editions, comment on contemporary life and frequently undertake light satire; but entertainment seems their primary concern. Sentimental personifications of flowers populate John Langhorne's *The Fables of Flora* (1771). Some of William Russell's *Fables Moral and Sentimental* (1772) derive directly from Aesop, but others bear only a tenuous relationship to the genre. Russell advertises, for the benefit of the more delicate, that he has assiduously avoided ''such creatures and things as are mean or disagreeable'' and has ''seldom made use of vermin, or domestic animals.'' [14]

Aside from volumes of traditional fables—retranslated, reworked, or merely reprinted—designed for children, the genre remained primarily a pastime in England. A "fable," moreover, might be any kind of professedly moral poem or tale, often presenting the moral as an afterthought to wit and amusement.

CHAPTER TEN

Herder and the Romantic Turn

Lessing's fable theory exercised a far-reaching influence in the German world, to the extent that subsequent commentators normally quote and often paraphrase it. Much of this influence undoubtedly derived from Lessing's overall stature as author and critic, rather than from exceptional brilliance in his treatment of the fable; even so, Lessing's stature was not lofty enough to intimidate determined opponents. We have already seen Bodmer's massive assault on Lessing's fable theory.

More serious attacks came from Johann Georg Hamann and especially from Johann Gottfried von Herder, both of them ideological and esthetic guides for the *Sturm und Drang,* the revolutionary movement of idealistic young German writers which helped foment the great period of German Classicism and Romanticism. In general Lessing himself represents a transition from strict neoclassic orthodoxy to new artistic forms and ideas. His treatment of the fable, however, is conservative to the point of reactionary, calling as it does for direct moral didacticism with no artistic adornment. Such ultraconservatism, especially from a man of Lessing's eminence, was sure to antagonize Herder, Hamann, and others of their persuasion who sought poetic beauty and shied away from rigid didacticism. Herder in particular had in mind a conception of the fable sharply at odds with the traditional didactic tool supported by Lessing. By the time he finished developing it, he had the fable well on its way from pedagogy toward folklore. At this point the history of the genre becomes a chapter in the controversy between Neoclassicism and Romanticism and in the transition from the one to the other.

Johann Georg Sulzer, whose pedagogical works were discussed in Chapter VIII, takes an initial step in the new direction. The article on fable in his *Allgemeine Theorie der schönen Künste (General Theory of the Fine Arts,* 1771–74), an encyclopedia of the arts, adheres to Lessing in many respects but significantly departs from him in others. Sulzer echoes his influential predecessor in his definition of the fable as "the narration of an occurred event insofar that it is a moral image" [1] and in his stress on narrative or plot rather than simple description. Like Lessing he asserts that the action must give the impression of factuality rather than just feasibility: depiction of a merely possible event instead of an "actual" occurrence results in an example, not a fable. Borrowing Lessing's terminology, he declares that the genre proposes "to present important concepts and notions to the intuitive understanding, vividly and with great esthetic force" (II, 165).

Sulzer emphasizes the high literary status of the fable and confutes those who relegate it to children's books: "The Aesopian fable is a work in which the aim of art is fulfilled in the most direct and forceful manner. It is in no way, as it is sometimes represented, an invention to impress the truth on children, but a sustenance also suited to the strongest manly intellect" (II, 165). Although remarking the existence of numerous critical studies of the genre, he doubts the pertinence or correctness of most and describes the fable, by way of explanation, as one of the most complex genres, both in regard to essence and to form.

Despite his various borrowings from Lessing, Sulzer contradicts him on essential matters. He regards a wondrous or strange ambience as an integral characteristic of the fable, an argument deriving from Breitinger which Lessing derided. Sulzer also ignores Lessing's principle that the genre should avoid touching the emotions. On the contrary, it so admirably accomplishes its instructive mission because it operates through the senses of the reader. All concepts, principles, and abstract truths, asserts Sulzer, become practical for a man only when he feels them. Since rational recognition does not suffice, the fable supplements the appeal to reason with a sensuous impression. Sulzer compares the method to the Spartan custom of parading drunken slaves before youths in order to impress upon them the degradation of drunkenness. He also stresses the function of genius in the creation of the fable and the venerability of the genre, which he calls one of the oldest "fruits of rhetorical genius" (II, 168). It was born of allegory— Sulzer again contradicts Lessing—and, together with its ancient parent, derives from the very earliest epoch of mankind, when language was not yet rich enough to express all thought. Allegory, including its fable offshoot, germinates naturally in a clever person, whether savage or civilized. The fable, thus common to all peoples, has no particular place of origin.

The notion of a primitive, anonymous provenience has been suggested by such predecessors of Sulzer as Addison and Batteux. Despite tradition, according to this notion, Aesop did not invent the genre—nor did Pilpai, Lockman, or any of the Eastern sages. Aesop's name became attached to the fable because his genius overwhelmed all earlier fabulists, but the form itself developed among all ancient peoples from man's innate powers of imagination and creativity. Once this primitive source has been established, the next step—taken by Herder—leads to interpretation of the fable as an expression of natural unity, signifying and deriving from a primeval "Golden Age" when all men, animals, and objects were bound together in a unified, comprehensive whole. Sulzer does not take this step, remaining closer to Lessing and the neoclassical principles of reason, regularity, and didacticism.

Even before Sulzer published his *Allgemeine Theorie,* however, Herder had begun rebelling against a concept of the fable based on didacticism and artificiality, which he saw represented by Lessing; and a foreboding of Herder's argument comes from Johann Georg Hamann. In a letter to his brother (12 April 1760) Hamann expresses his dissatisfaction, to put it mildly, with Lessing's fables and theoretical essays: "I have read Lessing's fables; the first book of them disgusted me. The beauty of nature seems to be transformed into gallantry. His essays are more boring than philosophical and witty to the end of agreeable instruction." [2] He defends La Fontaine against Lessing's sharp criticism, claiming that La Fontaine's loquacity derives from his individuality and his true narrative powers. Lessing, on the other hand, is nothing more than a "painter of miniatures" (III, 19–20). Although Lessing himself insists that fables must generate plot and action rather than rely on static description, Hamann scorns Lessing's own as a collection of stilted vignettes and accuses him not only of lacking La Fontaine's individuality and narrative ability but of having the audacity to criticize the French poet for possessing these qualities. He takes Lessing to task for disregarding nature and also discards his explanation for the use of animals, calling it whimsical and basically false. Hamann throws his own support to Breitinger's concept of wonder.

The fundamental ideological basis of his disagreement becomes clear when he equates Lessing's classically rooted ideas on the fable with Diderot's on drama—also classically oriented, according to Hamann—and concludes that both had "the will-o'-the-wisp of a false philosophy for guide." [3] Hamann, for whom neoclassic didacticism and artificiality are anathema, depicts poetry as the original language of mankind and demands that it be natural and spontaneous. If poetry is the original language, the fable is one of the earliest dialects. Hamann stresses the antiquity of the genre in a letter to Johann Gottfried Herder, in which he deliberates on classification of the poetic genres and concludes that "epos and fable is the beginning, and since then nothing but ode and song." [4]

In writing about the fable to Herder, Hamann spoke to an interested listener. Herder himself published several articles and commentaries on the genre, dating from about 1767 and continuing into the early years of the subsequent century; and although his ideas underwent minor mutations over this considerable span of time, he remained in consistent agreement with Hamann's notions about the importance of the fable in the primitive origins of language and literature. Herder, moreover, established a comprehensive critical and historical perspective for the genre, particularly in his article "On Image, Poetry, and Fable," and, transcending purely scholarly perceptions, created a kind of mystique of the fable by depicting it as an expression and symbol of the primeval natural unity which modern civilized man has lost.

Herder's earliest commentaries reflect Lessing, who, indeed, figures in all of his writings on the fable, either in the forefront as focus of discussion or in the background as provocation for his own dissenting insights. In an early piece, "On the Modern Use of Mythology," Herder defends contemporary use of classical mythology against denigrations that characterize it as nothing more than a composite of the errors and superstitions of the Ancients. He replies that classic myths provide adornment and illustration at the very least and considerably more in the case of instructive fables, "which make a certain general principle intuitively recognizable to us in a specific instance which is presented as real" [5]—a paraphrase of Lessing's definition. Not only do the classical fables remain eternally instructive, but their example continues to inspire modern fabulists, among whom Herder bestows his specific approval on Lessing, Gellert, Gleim, Lichtwer, and Hagedorn.

Although Herder's initial commentary touches on Lessing's fable theory only in passing, a subsequent essay, "Aesop and Lessing" (1767–68), undertakes a thorough analysis of it. Herder begins by commending Lessing, who has returned the fable to its "fatherland, instructive prose," and has reintroduced the brevity, simplicity, and philosophical sense of Aesop. [6] The praise rings sincere; but having granted it, Herder proceeds to a point-by-point analysis of Lessing's concepts, which, if it does not quite tear his theory to shreds, at least tends to qualify it to shreds.

Lessing describes the lesson inculcated by the fable as a "general moral principle"; Herder qualifies it to "general practical principle," explaining that "practical" still connotes *moral* but eliminates the suggestion of *abstract* which accompanies "general." To support his argument Herder refers to Aristotle, who specifies in his *Rhetoric* that the fable aims to convince the common people and, therefore, must deal with the daily, practical matters that concern them. Herder condemns the multitude of modern fables which forsake the living world and take refuge in the rarefied atmosphere of art, elegant society, or erudition.

Stressing the necessity of plot or action, which signifies a beginning, middle, and end, Herder remains dubious of Lessing's substitution of "instance." Without plot the fable degenerates into an "allegorical image" or "witty notion" (II, 193). Nor does Herder accept Lessing's claim that the genre uses animals because of their universally recognizable attributes. The fable must be simple and unadorned, qualities which Aesop's unexcelled examples best demonstrate; and animals possess an inherent simplicity which is unavoidably transferred to fables. There is always the danger of complexities ruinously encumbering fables that employ human or superhuman characters. Although not limiting the possibilities to beasts, Herder maintains their primacy both as the best and the most ancient characters for the fable.

Herder also confutes Lessing's denial of allegory in the fable, asserting that the very essence of the genre is comparison or allegory. Finally, he rejects Lessing's concept of intuitive knowledge or recognition, although previously having borrowed the term, and claims that it is a purely philosophical notion and a derivative of Lessing's misguided attempt to establish the fable in philosophy. The fable properly belongs on the border between philosophy and poetry, where, declares Herder, Aristotle also established it. But if forced to place it exclusively in one realm or the other, Herder would choose poetry: "its essence is invention; its life, plot; its aim, sensuous understanding . . . I regard the fable as a source, a miniature, of the great poetic genres, where most of the poetic rules are found in their original simplicity and, to a certain extent, in their original form" (II, 197–98). Lessing the fabulist, moreover, is poet—practicing the art of dialogue, polishing brevity to the pithy smoothness of epigram, exercising inventiveness—despite his own adamant disclaimer. In recompense, if such it can be called, Herder allows that Lessing's credentials as poet are inferior to Aesop's, whose degree of excellence he does not approach.

Despite the tenor of the article, Herder, subsequent to Lessing's death, composed a eulogy of him in which he accords high praise to his predecessor's fables and particularly to his theoretical work on the genre: "Without a doubt this is the most valid, steadily philosophical theory of a poetic genre produced since Aristotle's time." [7] Although recognizing objections both to Lessing's theory and fables, Herder denies the validity of Bodmer's *Lessingsche unäsopische Fabeln* and mitigates his own criticism of the fables, still maintaining their utter dissimilarity to Aesop's but now recognizing, in compensation, the dissimilarity of the epochs in which the two fabulists lived. Lessing's he calls "a more refined sort of Aesopian fable," written in response to contemporary demands (xv, 492). The popular or folk element suffers as a result of the heightened refinement, but Lessing himself is not to blame.

Herder's definitive treatment of the fable is the essay "On Image, Poetry, and Fable," published in the third collection of *Zerstreute Blätter* (1787). In the foreword Herder declares that some of the critical perceptions date back to 1767, when the material was quite original—but perhaps still is, he adds, "because since Lessing the theory of the fable, as far as I know, has not been further pursued" (xv, 517). Subsequent critics had adhered either to Lessing or to the Swiss Breitinger and Bodmer, failing in either case to produce original theory, a situation which Herder regrets: "for a reflective mind nothing is more beautiful than a neat theory, whatever it might concern" (xv, 517). The statement seems to indicate a rather curious penchant for theory for the sake of theory.

In the initial section of the essay, on image, Herder sets up a philosophical and psychological background for the operation of the fable. The only material that the reason has to work with, he declares, is accumulated by the senses, among which sight is dominant. The external object is transformed into an image in the individual mind; and this image is the vital factor in formulating thought, which, in turn, decides verbal and other expression. The fact that image forms in the individual mind means, for one thing, that all perceptions are individual. Secondly, the continual flow of images through the mind comprises an unceasing allegory, which is the essence of poetry; and thus, thoughts, language, and life itself are constructed on a poetic foundation: "Our entire life is, so to speak, a poetics: we do not see, rather we create images for ourselves. . . . Hence it follows that our soul, as well as our speech, continually allegorizes" (xv, 526).

Considered from the perspective of art, the notion of the individuality of perceptions means that all genuine artistic expression is individual and original. Herder scorns imitation and declares inexhaustible the possibilities for originality. Inner feeling provides the essential ingredient for art, as it does for all expression; and the only "rules" or criteria for judging it refer to its degree of truth, liveliness, and clarity.

The second part of the treatise, "On Poetry," begins by reiterating and amplifying the concept of original expression: "We compose poetry out of nothing but what we feel; just as with single images we transpose *our sense* into the objects, so with series of images our way of *invention* and thought; and this stamp of analogy, if it becomes art, we call poetry" (xv, 532–33). Man looks at surrounding nature and forms images in his mind; his expression derives from these images, which together form an analogy or individualized animation, formulated to make the "objective reality" comprehensible. Poetry, claims Herder, is essentially a personification of nature inspired by man's inability to perceive ultimate explanations for the powers that control the universe. Even a so-called empirical science such as physics is "a kind of poetics," derived from our experience (xv, 533); and the identical urge to provide explanations results in mythologies and religions. Herder adamantly declares that aside from this poetic personification man possesses no other means of deriving order and sense from his perceptions, which, conversely, defines poetry: "an attempt to explain the changes of the universe, its becoming, existence, and extinction. This it is for the most ignorant Negro and was for the cleverest Greek; the human spirit neither can, likes, nor desires to poeticize other than this'' (xv, 535). Culture signifies development of the crude allegorical perceptions, but both the head-hunting aborigine and the sophisticated Greek produce poetry because of their inability to comprehend.

Herder's avowal that all poetry involves the personification of nature opens a broad path directly to the fable, which he follows in the third section of the essay. The fable, like all poetry, derives from the natural human need to form images to create order out of the chaos of nature. Its distinctive characteristic is the moral lesson which the poet consciously incorporates into his perceptions. The type of characters utilized—whether gods, men, animals, or trees—does not affect the nature of the fable, which is simply "a moralized poem" (xv, 539).

Despite the eclectic assortment of characters admissible to the fable, Herder recognizes a traditional preference for animals and attempts to account for it. For the sensitive man all aspects of nature are potential actors, he asserts; but man maintains a closer relationship to animals than to any other segment of creation. Herder flatly rejects the notion that beasts are no more than "Cartesian machines," contending that all sensitive people feel a close bond to the animal world, especially to those species most resembling them and, therefore, most comprehensible to them. In general, animals lack only human organization and power of speech. Herder contravenes Breitinger's concept of wonder as an explanation for bestial characters, declaring that the animal fable harks back to a primal age of unity when man experienced a close bond to all other aspects of creation and could readily feel himself part of a unified whole. A lingering nostalgia for the lost age of unity explains the traditional introductory phrases "Once upon a time . . ." and "In the days when animals spoke . . ." Herder claims that children and the masses, to whom fables most particularly address themselves, never doubt the credibility of these historical allusions.

A similar explanation for the fable in a different context comes from *Vom Geist der Ebräischen Poesie* (*On the Spirit of Hebrew Poetry*, 1782), in which Herder depicts as the beginning of human wisdom God's marshaling of all the animals so that they could pass in review before Adam and Adam could name them: "The Deity thus presented in front of man a continuing Aesopian fable" (XI, 327). And from this divinely presented fable "man formed his strengths of contemplation, his skills at comparison and abstraction, his reason and speech" (XI, 326). In the second volume of the same work (1783), Herder returns to this primeval event and calls it "a school of fable" (XII, 12). Naming of the animals implies intimate knowledge of them, contends Herder, referring also to Eve's conversations with the snake. All this evidence indicates that from the earliest times man has been inextricably bound together with animals and that his original knowledge derives from them. Herder concludes, therefore, that the fable naturally became one of the first poetic genres.

Returning to the essay "On Image, Poetry, and Fable," Herder, having discarded Breitinger's wonder as an explanation for bestial characters, also reiterates his objection to Lessing's attempt to account for them by noting their universally recognizable characteristics. A minor factor, counters Herder, reasserting the primary importance of animals as an expression of the unity of man with all nature. He insists, moreover—again aiming at Lessing—that the effectiveness of the fable in inculcating a moral lesson derives from its reliance on tangibles as opposed to abstractions. This means that the fable is always based on concrete analogy or allegory. Lessing's distinction between simple and complex, therefore, has no validity, since all fables are complex due to their inherent allegory. A simple type does not exist; lacking allegory, the attempted fable degenerates into a vague, monotonous series of abstractions. Herder does caution, however, that the allegory must be "living"; it must be relevant and recognizable, avoiding convoluted and abstruse comparisons.

Having rejected Lessing's simple and complex, Herder brands irrelevant his further divisions, such as moral, mythical, and hyperphysical, all of them based on the type of personages employed. The fabulist can accomplish his purpose with any of a vast assortment of characters, providing only that the results fulfill the general requirements of "truth, liveliness, clarity" and that the invented narrative successfully inculcate the moral lesson. Categorization according to the type of characters employed, asserts Herder, serves no purpose.

In the last of his five essays Lessing had discussed possible applications of the fable in the classroom, promoting in particular the idea that the teacher take advantage of the opportunity which it offers to develop original thinking in the pupils. Herder seizes on the suggestion but rejects restriction of the exercise to abstract thought. He favors the cultivation of practical knowledge and thinking, particularly the training of students to transpose and apply the lesson learned from one situation to a parallel situation. Nor does he limit the possibilities of imaginative application only to moral precepts, noting that the great discoveries in all fields of knowledge are made by analogy. Herder doggedly adheres to his convictions about practical knowledge but still outlines a process of thought that demands abstraction—drawing lessons from one situation and applying them to another. All in all, his proposed classroom application of fables does not seem to differ significantly from Lessing's.

Having covered all five of Lessing's essays in the course of developing his own ideas on the fable, Herder moves toward a closing crescendo. Up to this point he has said relatively little about the didactic element—or perhaps *revelatory* element better suits Herder's interpretation—but it has a strong bearing on his peroration. He approaches the topic by comparing the fable with the example and the parable. Both of the latter two, he claims, are caught in something of a limbo between poetry and truth and lack the "intrinsic necessity" of the fable. All poetry can recommend or suggest, but only the fable insists and in a way that allows no refusal. This irresistibility stems from its connection with nature, both in regard to means and ends; and, as Herder interprets it, the means, the use of animal or other "natural" characters, becomes an end in itself. The fable animates the creatures of nature to serve as actors. They demonstrate for us "the *moral laws of the Creation* itself in their intrinsic necessity" (xii, 558). But animated nature speaking to us also gives us a lesson in fundamental unity, which primitive man felt so strongly that it guided every aspect of his life but which modern man, alienated from nature, only dimly senses. Thus, as Herder sees it, both the lesson of the fable and the fable itself as a representation of natural unity assume sublime proportions. He concludes the essay by underscoring this double significance: the fable teaches *"higher, universal laws of nature,"* and it demonstrates *"the immutable union of all beings in the empire of the Creation"* (xii, 559). A fable which fails to achieve this sublimity is not a fable at all but a parable, an example, or simply an amusing story.

In addition to providing his theory of the fable, Herder's discussions aim to rebut Lessing. Much of the difference between their notions of the fable suggest the difference between the neoclassical man of reason and the romantic follower of feeling and inspiration. Lessing's insistence on a short and stark didactic piece clashes with Herder's temperament and ideology. However, by the time that Herder finishes formulating his exalted conception, the composition of fables by mere mortals seems virtually out of the question. It would seem more proper to climb a mountain and receive them burned into stone tablets. In Herder's hands the fable is no longer a simple didactic tale, nor even the more sophisticated moral poetry of La Fontaine. It transmits something approaching divine revelation set in a formula which reflects a mythological golden age of cosmic unity.

A few years later, in the foreword to a collection of instructive tales, *Erlesene morgenländische Erzählungen für die Jugend* (*Selected Oriental Tales for Young People,* 1787), Herder seems to undermine his elevated concept of the fable as an expression of the ultimate truths of nature. He still recommends Aesop's fables but asserts that the potential of the genre is limited: "Not every lesson needed for youth can be put in the mouth of an animal or be expressed by his behavior" (xvi, 586). The remark calls to mind Bodmer's similar avowal of the inherent limitations of animal characters. Herder further claims that those exceeding bestial capabilities include the "noblest, essential lessons" (xvi, 586). Adaptation of beasts to such sublime pedagogical purpose would require excessive humanizing of them, and the fable would lose force and charm as a result. For more advanced instruction, Herder now recommends the oriental tale, which combines simplicity, noble style, attractive exoticism, and a clear moral lesson but which avoids the complexities causing most stories dealing with human characters to go over the heads of children.

In spite of these comments, Herder's esteem for the fable apparently remained basically intact. In 1801 he provided the journal *Adastrea* with a further treatment of the genre, which essentially repeats the earlier "On Image, Poetry, and Fable" as far as theory goes. Its setting within a framework of lamentations over the decay of the fable, however, and its repeated pleas for generic renewal mark it as a product of the ensuing generation. This final essay of Herder's will, therefore, be discussed in a later chapter.

Herder was by no means the only one asserting the antiquity of the fable and interpreting it as an expression of natural unity. These notions began to reflect the mainstream of thought on the genre; and they were frequently accompanied by depiction of the fabulist as a "natural" genius or sometimes as a "child of nature"—shunning civilized society, incorporating himself into the natural environment, reviving and reliving the sense of unity discernable at the fable's ancient source. A common denominator of many late eighteenth-century discussions of the fable is steady deemphasis of the consciously didactic element. The fable still teaches, but interpretations now perceive the lesson as deriving directly from universal nature rather than from the religious or social moral code. The lesson, moreover, tends to be pervasive rather than defined, no longer suitable for expression in a succinct moral tag.

Johann Wolfgang von Goethe provides a glimpse of his own notion of the genre in the process of criticizing a volume of fables and stories by H. Braun for the periodical *Frankfurter gelehrte Anzeigen*

(1772). Braun had advised that young people could advantageously follow his structural precepts and use his fables as examples in order to compose ones of their own. Goethe derisively seconds the advice, recommending the precepts and examples not only for "vicious youths" but also for all others "who venture into this field without genius." [8] Admonishing that talented fabulists will derive little assistance from Braun, however, he launches a brief recital of the origin and development of the fable, condemning the oppressive sway of rules and reason in the process.

Goethe asserts that the fable originated in primitive times as a vehicle for folk wisdom. Early man employed examples to teach and convince. With the arrival of a time when true examples no longer carried sufficient force, he began to invent them. Thus, poetry was born. Poets began calling upon animals because "a fiction which says no more than what the eye sees is always insipid" (xxxvii, 220). The original, untrained fabulist depended on his native powers of invention; and this was the case until men "began to reason more than to live" (xxxvii, 220). Rigid literary rules and stereotyped plots fossilized the fable, eliminating the possibility of originality and even of genuine instruction. Fabulists operating under these conditions made fables into frivolous poetic ornaments. They decorated and refined them until the original instructive form was distorted into an impotent mixture of fable and story, aiming only to amuse. It was noticed how far the genre had degenerated from the vigorous original, and efforts at renewal attempted to purge the ornamental excesses; but they went no further than to inject it with mere wit. As a result the fable became epigram. This sketch, declares Goethe, indicates the history of fable theory as he would write it. He once again vents his utter scorn of the volume under review but concludes on a note of cynical tolerance: "Why should Herr. B. not have as much right to poeticize and to theorize as others?" (xxxvii, 220).

In a series of terse and sometimes enigmatic comments on the fable collected in his *Fragmente,* the German Romantic poet Novalis emphasizes the antiquity and universality of the genre. He describes it in terms that suggest the mystical qualities of a divine oracle—for example, the lesson which it inculcates: "The lesson of the fable contains the history of the archetypal world; it comprises antiquity, present, and future." [9] The fable is "the apogee of the poetic, popular statement of philosophy of the first period—or philosophy in the natural state." In this early period it was not poetry but "philosophy become poetry" (p. 668). Novalis seems to say that the fable still does not quite belong to belles-lettres. He calls it "technical," based on a purpose and aiming for a definite goal, qualities alien to pure art. In this "first period" from which the fable derives, however, all forms of communication and expression were one and the same, becoming differentiated only later. Novalis asserts that the earliest art was hieroglyphics, which helps to elucidate his theory of the primeval unity of all forms of expression. He also explains the fabulist's uninhibited freedom of personification as deriving from a sense of pantheism: "For this age reason and deity do not speak clearly, not strikingly enough, out of a man; stones, trees, and animals must speak in order to make man feel himself and think of himself" (p. 669). The fable, therefore, as Novalis perceives it, seems to be a combination of the primal hieroglyphical expression and pantheistic outlook.

A nature-oriented concept of the fable was also becoming prevalent in France. Claude Joseph Dorat, for example, envisions the fabulist as residing in the seclusion of a rustic environment and drawing inspiration from his surroundings. In "Reflections on Fables," prefaced to his collection *Fables ou allégorie philosophiques,* he pictures the German fabulists as having realized this ideal. Admitting that he has borrowed from Hagedorn and Gellert for his own fables, Dorat praises German writers in general for a simplicity of ways that perfectly suits the fable and credits them with placing poetry "on the very throne of nature." [10] The rustic setting, nature, animals, all of them serve as "subjects of meditation for those tranquil philosophers, who rise slowly from observations of the physical world to grand speculations of morality" (III, 121–22). The fable, more than any other genre, flourishes under these conditions, "in the middle of the flocks, in the silence of the woods" (III, 122).

Dorat endows the fable with a touch of rebelliousness by declaring that it was born of the combat between liberty of thought and fear of displeasing. It forms a veil "of which the truth takes advantage in order to tame the ego and attack tyranny" (III, 111). But Dorat, although calling his a corrupt century, has no stomach for revolution and warns that direct attacks on vices and pretensions run the risk of provoking one. Indeed, therein lies the distinct advantage of the fable: "I regard it as a mid-point between license to say all and cowardly silence. As I see it, it is mitigated satire" (III, 122).[11]

La Fontaine, says Dorat, was a free man, at liberty to speak out, but timid and uncommunicative; he therefore developed the fable into a means of expressing his ideas. Of the two kinds of talent Dorat recognizes, one based on instinct and the other on reflection, La Fontaine's, in his opinion, was decidedly the former—"the instinct of nature itself" (III, 122), manifested in a brilliant simplicity—and Dorat effuses soaring praise for his fables. After writing off Richer as an insignificant imitator, he grants La Motte high marks for his discourse but characterizes his fables as defective. La Motte, a born philosopher who insisted on being a poet, constructed fables pure in form and morality but lacking in poetic sense and grace. Lessing, on the other hand, receives praise and censure in inverse proportions: Dorat exalts him with the title "the Aesop of Germany" but chafes at his pedantic, long-winded theories and explanations—"his eternal prefaces" (III, 120).

Neoclassic critics normally define the fable as a didactic narrative, while later ones, in the trend toward Romanticism, frequently interpret it as an expression of natural unity or truth. Guillaume-Antoine Le Monnier despairs of defining the fable at all and ultimately declares the impossibility of doing so. In "On the Fable," prefaced to his *Fables, contes et épitres,* he begins by asking the question, "what is the fable?" [12] In the attempt to arrive at an answer, he first summarizes the various meanings of the term—e.g., narrative, literary plot, pagan mythology—and then turns to La Motte's definition, which, as he acknowledges, concerns the *Aesopian* fable, his own specific concern in this essay. But he doubts the comprehensiveness of La Motte's definition, "an instruction disguised under the allegory of an action." He complains that it ignores fables devoid of action, allegory, or moral, nor does it provide for those constructed in the form of dialogue. All of these gaps in the definition suggest the advisability of discarding it—and the same criticism, argues Le Monnier, applies to every one that has been proposed. The formulation of a single definition applicable to all fables would demand a firm code of rules for their construction, which does not exist, nor does anyone have the right to fabricate one. Aesop created his fables without benefit of rules or models, nor did Phaedrus, asserts Le Monnier, feel obliged to imitate his predecessor; and La Fontaine, illustrating the same ingenuity in more contemporary times, produced masterpieces without rules or emulation of his forerunners. Each of these masters in the genre simply followed his own genius, which is the only way of creating true literature and the only "rule" which can reasonably be prescribed for the fabulist, or any poet.

Le Monnier refers to La Motte as an example: all his rules seem well considered, reasonable, and valid—until one finds them broken by a true genius, such as La Fontaine, and perceives their irrelevancy. Nor do La Motte's own fables, carefully constructed according to his rules, measure up to La Fontaine's, which conform to nothing but their creator's genius. Le Monnier censures as equally unjustified, however, the practice of regarding La Fontaine's fables as the rule book for the genre and consequently of condemning any that do not adhere to his example. He insists that the fable is a ground as fertile and open to cultivation in his own time as it was in Aesop's day.[13]

A parallel notion of original genius giving birth to the fable, accompanied by the lavish praise of La Fontaine which by the latter part of the eighteenth century had become commonplace, appears in the narrative essay "On the Fable" with which Jean Pierre Claris de Florian introduces his collection. Florian, however, limits instinctive genius to the fable, maintaining the validity of rules in other genres. The narrative essay commences with Florian accompanying a friend on a visit to the latter's octogenarian uncle, who, it turns out, has been a life-long enthusiast of the fable. At the request of the old man

Florian reads a dozen of his own fables, which meet with approval; and a discussion of the genre ensues. Asked about his theory, the fabulist shamefacedly admits that he has never seriously considered the conceptual aspect; but the old man relieves his discomfort by undertaking to explain his own theory, which concentrates on the distinguishing characteristic of the fable: "This genre is perhaps the only one in which poetics are almost useless, in which study adds almost nothing to talent. . . . One composes by a kind of instinct." [14] Other genres, such as epic, comedy, and the novel, have rules which can guide the novice writer to excellence; but the fable achieves excellence only by being perfectly told, or *bien faite,* a quality that transcends all rules. The octogenarian selects La Motte as an example, as did Dorat and Le Monnier, admonishing that the would-be fabulist could abide by his definitions and follow his rules to the letter and still produce mediocre fables. He then borrows Marmontel's terms *"bonhomme"* and "credulous simplicity" to help depict the instinctive, essentially undefinable qualities of a successful fabulist, perorating his argument with raptures on La Fontaine. Poor Florian, overcome with discouragement, attempts to throw his own fables into the fire; but the old man restrains him, reassuring the disheartened fabulist that despite La Fontaine's incomparable example there are still excellent, if lesser, positions available in the hierarchy of fabulists. Judging by what the old man said previously, the despairing poet could change over to tragedy, study the rules and examples, and hope for excellence. But first-rate fabulists are born, not made.

Herder, as we have seen, imbues the fable with a revelatory or prophetic message and derives the form from the primeval past of the human race. He has no use for the traditional reliance on rules and didacticism, for him personified by Lessing. The Frenchmen Dorat, Le Monnier, and Florian concur insofar as they reject the following of strict rules, as exemplified by La Motte. The fabulist *par excellence* is the inspired genius, who is beyond all rules and imitation. In either case, the fable has ceased to be a simple didactic narrative to illustrate a moral. It takes genius to produce one, and the lesson now seems to require a Delphic aura.

CHAPTER ELEVEN

Samaniego, Iriarte, and the Fable in Spain

The history of the fable in eighteenth-century Spain, considered strictly on the basis of Spanish contributions to the genre, consists of little more than a footnote to its development and practice elsewhere. Nor, which is pertinent to this study, did any Spanish critic of the era attempt a theoretical treatment. In an incomparably barren century for Spanish literature, on the other hand, the fable obtrudes as one of the few areas in which there was any verdant growth, chiefly the attainment of Tomás de Iriarte with his original and poetically creative *Fábulas literarias* (*Literary Fables*), which were accorded the distinction of translation into all major European languages. Fables, and again Iriarte's in particular, also constitute a landmark in the belated introduction of neoclassical ideas into Spain. Considering the situation, therefore, the fable might have had a greater actual impact in Spain, arriving as it did on a scene of intellectual and literary sterility, than in France, Germany, and England, where as a minor genre it was dwarfed by significant accomplishments in the major ones.

By the time that Félix María Samaniego published the first part of his *Fábulas en verso castellano* (*Fables in Castilian Verse*) in 1781, the genre had long been a medium for original expression in France and Germany. Samaniego contemplates no more than a reworking of traditional fables, declaring in the prologue to his collection that such has been the respectable task of all fabulists since Aesop.[1] In his expanded 1784 collection, however, he does include a section of original fables, probably produced under the stimulus of Iriarte's success. Samaniego directs his fables to a youthful audience, specifically the students at the Real Seminario Bascongado, and strives for clarity and simplicity, qualities which, he remarks, La Fontaine often lacks. He purposely composes in a variety of meters, maintaining that verse serves as a mnemonic aid and that a variety of it holds attention and contributes to the cultivation of the ear. These comments on the pedagogical employment of fables, including the criticism of La Fontaine for lack of simplicity and clarity, reflect numerous previous discussions which we have considered, although they are apparently fresh material in Spain. Samaniego makes note of his extensive study of the genre, both theories and fables, prior to undertaking his own compositions.

Samaniego respectfully dedicates the third book of the first volume to Don Tomás de Iriarte, who published his own *Fábulas literarias* in 1782, a year later. Iriarte's is a considerably more ambitious undertaking than Samaniego's, since he not only creates original fables but relates them all to literature by having them give advice to aspiring writers and warn of literary pitfalls—a difficult task, comments Iriarte's editor, since the animal characters neither read nor write.[2] Iriarte composes his fables, moreover, in forty varieties of poetic meter, indexed at the end of the volume. Both literary principles and metric examples derive from neoclassical sources, and the collected fables therefore represent a writer's handbook for neoclassical literature.[3] Iriarte thus transforms the traditional moral didacticism of the fable into a literary or esthetic didacticism.

Iriarte attained considerable renown both as poet and ideologist. A German translation of his fables appeared in 1784, only two years after the original; and a review of the translation in the periodical *Der deutsche Merkur* praises Iriarte as one of the most significant young Spanish writers and describes his *Literarische Fabeln* as "a catechism for writers and readers."[4] The French fabulist Florian, discussed in the foregoing chapter, admits to having borrowed freely from his predecessors and especially from Iriarte, "poet whom I esteem highly

and who has furnished me with my most successful apologues." [5] The
Fábulas literarias apparently underwent three separate translations
into English.[6]

The success of Iriarte's fables significantly reinforced his position
as one of the Spanish literary elite; but the *Fábulas literarias* also
provided a convenient focus for critical and personal attacks by opponents. The most vigorous and damaging assault was executed by Juan
Pablo Forner in the form of an "original fable," *El Asno erudito* (*The
Erudite Ass*, 1782), which appeared in the same year as Iriarte's fables
to disrupt the acclaim that the collection drew. Forner published the
caustic satire anonymously, inventing an editor who claims to have ac-
cidentally discovered a seventeenth-century manuscript. The ass in the
title role is a braying pedant intended to represent Iriarte, although the
fabulist never receives mention by name. There is no doubt of the reference, however, when the author scoffs at the claim that composition
of fables "is a very difficult business," replying that anyone with talent can do it—talent counts, not rules.[7] A bad poet, moreover, is bad
enough, he continues; but one with the audacity to make models and
precepts of his abominable creations adds stupidity to lack of talent
(pp. 62 ff.). And the work proceeds in this vein. After an apparent attempt to buy up all copies of *El Asno erudito* immediately after its appearance, Iriarte maintained silence for a time and then replied under
the pseudonym Geta. In this guise he admitted the personal reference
of the satire, which the literary public had immediately recognized,
and denounced the work as libel. As a result of the virulent attack,
factions began to coalesce behind Forner and Iriarte—the former, as
one critic describes him, emotional and even violent, temperamentally
inclined toward the incipient pre-Romanticism; the latter, proud and
haughty, representing the aristocracy and the classical sentiment.[8]

Samaniego, meanwhile, had joined the attack on Iriarte. Despite
having dedicated part of his 1781 collection to his fellow fabulist and
apparently having submitted the fables for his approval before publication, Samaniego penned a diatribe which was published under the in-
nocuous title "Observations on the Original Literary Fables of Don

Tomás de Iriarte."[9] In this work he derides Iriarte's *ars poetica* contained in his fables as a pale imitation of Horace's and ridicules his precepts for being obvious or stupid or both. Iriarte's dictation of artistic taste and style, moreover, stems from nothing more than overbearing presumption, since he himself lacks both. Samaniego labels insulting the employment of simple animals to talk to people dedicated to letters but maliciously remarks the suitability of Iriarte's style for the baseness of his chosen characters.

Samaniego avers that fable writing, more than any other poetic enterprise, demands inherent genius rather than acquired talent: "This genre requires not so much a great talent as a genius suited to it. If it is said that the poet is born, with much more reason it should be said of the fabulist, since he is born such and has almost nothing to learn."[10] Finding Iriarte, as one would expect, devoid of the requisite genius, Samaniego somewhat mitigates the condemnation by declaring La Fontaine to be the only genuine fabulist among all the modern poets who have aspired to the title. Iriarte, therefore, seems to stand with a multitude of other would-be fabulists who lacked the necessary genius. But Samaniego immediately prostrates his rival once again by unfavorably comparing his fables with La Motte's, which in themselves epitomize failure in the genre: La Motte "was a man of vast literary knowledge, the most brilliant talent of his nation and the idol of all gatherings; he wanted to follow in the footsteps of his countryman La Fontaine, and what happened? They made fun of his work. Nevertheless, his fables are infinitely superior to those of Señor Iriarte" (p. 132). He further calls La Motte's fables a monument to the difficulties of the genre and a warning to those of little talent imprudent enough to dedicate themselves to it.

Iriarte's reaction to Samaniego's piece of vitriol was an apparent attempt, through his brother's influence, to have judicial proceedings initiated against the author of the "Observations" on the grounds that publication of the treatise without specifying place or date violated the law.[11]

The controversy continued for several years, the factions hurling repeated insults at each other, none of the participants emerging with his integrity unblemished. The dispute about the relative merits and debilities of the *Fábulas literarias* seems to have endured, moreover, to the present day. Iriarte's reputation suffered an understandable decline during the period of Romantic ascendance, when the neoclassical doctrine found little following among the literary elite. In the latter years of the nineteenth century, however, Iriarte seems to have been called up for re-evaluation. Emilio Cotarelo y Mori's *Iriarte y su época* (1897) praises his fables and perceives a subtle satire of various contemporary personages, including Samaniego, in the depiction of the animals. Cotarelo y Mori explains the virulence of the attacks on Iriarte as due to the success of the fables and dismisses Forner's *El Asno erudito* as unmerited libel. As recently as 1961 Russell Sebold, in *Tomás de Iriarte: Poeta de "Rapto Racional"* (*Tomás de Iriarte: Poet of "Rational Ecstasy"*), expresses guarded admiration for the fabulist and calls for a more sympathetic appraisal of him, noting that recurring condemnations of his fables usually prove to be borrowed or derived from Forner and his vituperous cohorts.

CHAPTER TWELVE

Dissolution of a Functioning Literary Genre

Remarks suggesting the decay of the fable as an active literary genre have been noted earlier. The Abbé Aubert, writing at mid-century, pointedly stressed its continued viability, suggesting that certain of his contemporaries had declared otherwise. Lessing based his entire treatment of the genre on the contention that it had degenerated into a pretty poetical toy under the influence of La Fontaine, and he called for revitalization by returning to the original Aesopian model. In the closing years of the eighteenth century and the early years of the nineteenth such laments become frequent to the point of commonplace in commentaries on the fable. Concomitantly, both these commentaries and published volumes of fables become fewer. Interest in the genre rapidly wanes to the point where, as we shall see, those few who concern themselves with it tend to treat it historically, as a dead literary form no longer cultivated.

Johann Gottfried von Herder's interest in and high esteem for the fable was discussed at length in Chapter x. In an 1801 article printed in the journal *Adrastea,* Herder reasserts his lofty estimation, calling the fable ''a textbook of nature.'' [1] He appends, however, an admonitory qualification to this definition: such is the way that all nature-oriented peoples regard the fable. In his own degenerate time the genre has lost its supreme instructive function and its deserved prestige: ''Haughty times degrade everything; thus the great teacher of nature and educator of mankind, the fable, gradually became a gallant chat-

terer or a childish fairy-tale'' (XXIII, 255). La Fontaine, however in-
nocently, instigated the gradual disintegration by transforming the
fable into pure poetry. The French fabulist himself was a ''naive child
of nature''; but his multiple imitators, unable to maintain a balance between nature and art, so overrefined the genre that it became a ''finely
cut, dead paper flower'' (XXIII, 256). Thus this authentic nature poetry
degenerated into an amusing pastime and ultimately, through surfeit,
lost even that inferior function so that it no longer even amuses.

Herder brings up the possibility of generic renewal, which would
require restoration of the fable to its original focus on nature; and he
declares that renewal is not only possible but indispensable. No matter
how refined and sophisticated man fancies himself, he lives ''in the
hands as well as in the empire of nature'' and can never wrest himself
from her, no matter how hard he tries. Man needs the lessons which
the pure, nature-oriented fable can provide him. This wisdom is in-
valuable in the practical concerns of life, even in dealing with matters
of greatest importance: ''Who of us do not consider how often in our
lives, and to our own detriment in a moment of action, we lack the
memory of just one fable?'' (XXIII, 258). Nor is the fable literarily ex-
pendable, since as the simplest kind of poetry it forms the basis of all
poetry.

The remainder of the article essentially reiterates Herder's previous discussions of the genre; even the approach is the same, employing Lessing as focus and both praising and censuring his ideas. Herder
does introduce a tripartite system of classification. ''Theoretical'' fables, which deal with the laws of nature, are the purest and most eminent kind. ''Moral'' ones concern worldly matters such as love and
ambitions, and the ''destiny or demonic'' category, the working of
fate among human beings (XXIII, 263 ff.). Herder also gives guarded
stress to the comic element, which is essential but which must be
''high comic''—not the loud laugh that misguided contemporary fabulists attempt to arouse.

Although an inveterate advocate and admirer of the fable, Herder
perceives the unmistakable decay of the genre, which he associates

with pervasive social degeneration. He calls for renewal, hoping that a revitalized fable—the "textbook of nature"—will help to stem the tide carrying man away from nature and to awaken in him an awareness of his proper position in the world.

In Chapter x note was made of the young Goethe's assessment of the fable situation, expressed in the course of an acerbic review of a volume of them. He considered the fable an ingenious invention of primitive, nature-oriented man which had been perverted to a stereotyped poetical trifle by modern practitioners. Whereas Herder laments the dissipation of a valuable and favorite literary genre, however, the mature Goethe, reviewing eighteenth-century literary activities in *Dichtung und Wahrheit* (1812), expresses amazement at the attention given the little fable by so many of the German literary elite. In the process of discussing the ideological ferment in the first half of the century, he turns to Breitinger's concept of wonder and the prevailing demand for moral utility in literature, thereby arriving at the Aesopian fable: "However curious such a diversion might seem to us now, it certainly had the most decisive influence on the best minds. That Gellert and afterwards Lichtwer dedicated themselves to this specialty, that even Lessing attempted to work in it, that so many others turned their talents to it, speaks for the trust which this genre had won for itself." [2] Goethe obviously does not share that trust, nor does he expect his readers to do so. Far from taking up Herder's cry for renewal of the fable, he seems somewhat at a loss to explain the eighteenth-century interest in it.

Indications of the disintegration of the fable as an active literary genre and of its retreat into obscurity are not confined to Germany. Antoine Vincent Arnault, who was one of the last fabulists in the dedicated, eighteenth-century significance of the title, prefaced an 1812 collection with an essay "On the Fable." The beginning of the essay is a memorable example of the negative approach to a subject: "There remain few things to say about the apologue. . . . Finally, thanks to the panegyrists, to the commentators, to the imitators of La Fontaine, the dissertations on this genre of literature have so multiplied that the material seems almost exhausted.'' [3] However, Arnault recovers from his despair and finds something to say. He provides a brief history of the genre, beginning with Biblical examples, and summarizes selected theoretical ideas which he has inherited, such as the delineation of naiveté as the supreme quality of a fabulist. He defines the fable as a comparison but denies the common notion that it disguises the truth. On the contrary, it brightly illuminates the truth and in such a comprehensible way that he calls it the easiest way to express an idea. In addition to high regard for the genre, and despite his initial qualms about something to say, Arnault shows an irrepressible urge to expound. Lacking pertinent comments about the fables themselves, he disgorges multiple peripheral bits of information in the one hundred pages of notes appended to the volume. A fleeting reference to Switzerland, for example, elicits an explanatory note which includes a short history of the nation, a list of the twenty-two cantons, and a review of the contemporary Swiss political situation.

Whereas the foregoing essay suggests exhaustion of possibilities for further fable theory, a subsequent one by Arnault directs similar misgivings at the fable itself: ''Is it Necessary to Create Fables After La Fontaine?'' The mere selection of such a title would seem to indicate frequent negative replies to the question, although Arnault himself defends pursuance of the genre against such defeatism. Affirming the inexhaustibility of fertile subject matter, he claims that fresh attempts are always justified as long as they manage to strike out over untrodden terrain and to avoid following in the footsteps of predecessors. In any case, the great principles of morality are timeless and universal, he declares, and must be continually taught. Moreover, writing for people in any epoch, ''three-quarters of the time is not that writing for children? Write at least in order that they stop being such, if it is at all possible.'' [4] And, in a certain roundabout way, the fable once again finds itself classified as children's literature—for children of all ages, which include the majority of mankind.

Contemporary with Arnault, a certain Vincent-Augustin Fribault wrote a dissertation *De l'apologue* (1817), which undertakes a histori-

cal study of the genre. Concentrating on French practitioners and
theoreticians, he gives particular attention to the conceptual notions of
La Motte, Richer, and Batteux, finding the latter's most valid and
exact. However, Fribault's study is exclusively historical. He respects
the fable as a legitimate literary genre but leaves the unmistakable impression that it is dead. Designating La Fontaine's work the culmination of achievement in the genre, he dates the commencement of its
decline subsequent to the French master. By his own time, infers
Fribault, the fable has ceased to be a living genre, despite the lingering
efforts of such as Arnault.

   Much of the inspiration for eighteenth-century fable writing came
from La Fontaine. He set an example for modern fabulists in proving
that the Ancients could be challenged on their own ground, and there
were few during the century who did not rank him on a par with
Aesop and Phaedrus. On the other hand, La Motte was both the pace-
maker for fable theory and the example for composition of original
fables. There were comments on the genre before his, mainly prefaces
to collections; but his "Discourse" was the first attempt at a thorough
analysis and precise definition of the fable. Subsequent theoreticians
often begin with consideration of it in formulating their own ideas. It
could even be said that the fable's tenure as a viable literary genre
begins with La Motte, due both to his theorizing and to his volume of
original fables. Prior to his *Fables nouvelles* serious fabulists normally
translated and reworked the traditional ones associated with Aesop and
passed on by his successors. Even La Fontaine considered his own
productions to be translations of Phaedrus, who, in turn, had ran-
sacked Aesop in order to produce his own collection.
   Under this primary influence of La Fontaine and La Motte, the
century experienced an outburst of fable writing, especially in France
and Germany; and the hundreds of published volumes were accompanied by multiple treatises on the genre and overall enhancement of
its literary status. Earlier poetics, such as Boileau's *L'Art poëtique*,
normally omit the Aesopian fable, using the term in the broad sense of

literary plot or narrative. Such theoreticians as Gottsched, Breitinger, and Batteux, on the other hand, regard the Aesopian fable as one of the four standard literary genres.

The bulk of theoretical works on the fable derives from the middle fifty years of the century, when didacticism and strict literary rules were still accepted and even exalted but when the limitations imposed by inflexible worship of the Ancients had been relaxed, allowing modern writers room for individuality and chances of excellence. At one end of the stream of theoretical treatments there is La Motte and at the other, Herder. Herder's 1801 article laments the decay of the genre; but even the earlier "On Image, Poetry, and Fable" marks, to a great extent, the termination of both original fables and theoretical formulations. Herder probably did not intend his to be the final word; but his concept of the fable as a somewhat oracular expression of natural law and unity and his emphasis on its venerability tend to exclude conscious didacticism and thereby to inhibit pedagogical application. His elimination of literary rules and reliance on the undefined guidelines "truth, liveliness, and clarity" both hinder subsequent theoretical discussion and make further creation of fables a somewhat conjectural matter—except for the intuitive genius. All in all, Herder's notions tend to edge the fable into mythology or folklore, where the Romantics established it, and thereby to alter its function. Earlier theoreticians—Gellert, for example—declared that the fable addressed its instructive message to the "folk" or masses. Herder, on the other hand, construes the fable as *deriving* its wisdom from the "folk," in the sense that it conveys the folk wisdom of unsophisticated, nature-oriented man.

Looked at from another perspective, the traditional didacticism of the fable tended to be considered oppressive as the reigning ideology underwent a transformation and belief in the supremacy of reason gave way to respect for the workings of intuition. The efficacy of the form as a pedagogical tool, based on an appeal to reason, thus became questionable. The Romantics commonly regarded the fable as part of the general body of folklore, which they held in considerable esteem; but they had little interest in its didactic potential, other than in the oracular sense of a "textbook of nature." Nor did the rigid classical formula endear it to them. Despite the lingering residue of esteem deriving from its folkloric associations, the prestige of the fable steadily sank to a level where common opinion considered it to be a form of children's literature, precisely where it normally had been located in the seventeenth century prior to its climb to the status of a literary genre. And thus Goethe's rather bemused remark in *Dichtung und Wahrheit* (1812), questioning why the best literary minds in Germany had concerned themselves with the little fable—even though he himself, in his younger days, had been sufficiently interested to sketch a theory of its origin and to remark on its degeneration.

The fable found favor in the eighteenth century because it combined literary attractiveness with moral instruction. Nobody has ever doubted but that the fable should instruct, in some way or other. But that "some way or another" and the exact relationship of didacticism to the fable have been enduring points of contention among fable critics and theoreticians. The contention first arises with Lessing, who lamented the breach between the didactically pure Aesopian style and the poetically adorned La Fontainian. Theoreticians prior to Lessing normally prescribed a balance of moral lesson and artistic embellishment, warned against the latter overwhelming the former, but seemed willing to allow considerable leeway in poetic touches as long as the moral struck home loud and clear.

A contemporary critic takes Lessing's criticism of the La Fontainian innovations even further and claims that the French fabulist killed the genre. In an essay "On Iriarte, La Fontaine, and Fabulists in General" [5] Alejandro Cioranescu declares that the Ancients, who regarded poetry as a search for truth, invented the fable to serve as a philosophical or pedagogical tool, a purpose which it continued to serve through the Middle Ages. In the modern period, however, poetry has become dissevered from philosophical inquiry; and literary didacticism has become increasingly repugnant. Modern tastes demand escapism instead of moral lessons. Cioranescu asserts that La Fontaine, a product of the modern age, transformed the fable into poetry of the escapist variety, thereby dealing it a fatal blow. Subsequent fabulists imitated La Fontaine and drained the remaining life from the already stricken genre. Cioranescu claims that of all the multitude of post-La Fontaine fabulists only Iriarte, although not a great poet, managed to inject originality into the depleted traditional formula. His innovations were only a temporary reprieve, however, in the steady decline toward death.

Jacob Grimm fixes the incipient deterioration of the fable centuries earlier, even prior to Aesop. Contrary to Cioranescu, however, he ascribes it to "purification" of the genre for didactic purposes rather than to artistic dilution of the didacticism. In the essay "Essence of the Animal Fable," prefaced to *Reinhart Fuchs* (1834), his version of the renowned medieval animal epic, Grimm declares that the fable, like the epic, is inherently instructive but originally and properly so in conformity with nature, which means that it displays more vice than virtue. Adaptation to the purposes of moral didacticism meant tipping the balance in favor of virtue, which distorts observable nature and, therefore, marks the decline of the form. Since this didactic adaptation took place prior to Aesop, it seems that any examples of these original, nature-true fables would have to be found in oral folklore. Grimm's is essentially the Romantic point of view. As he sees it, La Fontaine worked at the tail end of a tradition long debilitated and perverted; and in any case, La Fontaine's poetical accomplishments have long been overrated. Nor does Grimm give much credit to Lessing's campaign to rescue the fable from the poetic excesses of La Fontaine and his followers: Lessing mistook Aesop's unadorned didacticism for the culmination of the genre rather than for the earlier deterioration that it really was.

Grimm's view conflicts, of course, with the usual estimations of Aesop and La Fontaine—especially the latter, who has even been credited with introducing the "Golden Age of the Fable." [6] It also virtually erases the fable from the list of workable literary genres and sets it in folklore. In so doing Grimm makes explicit what Herder implies. Written literature and a primitive, nature-oriented outlook tend to exclude each other. At best, one could hope for a clever imitation of the real fable.

A contemporary commentator, Ben Edwin Perry, refutes Grimm's interpretation of the didactic fable as a corruption of the animal story, and at the same time he provides a simplified explanation for the fable's literary decline at the end of the eighteenth century. The genre, he claims, has always been didactic. If it can be said to have been perverted, the perversion lies in the attempt to make poetry of it: "Fable in the hands of a highly competent stylist and a man of superior taste and intelligence, like *La Fontaine* or *Horace,* may qualify as first-class literature and even as poetry, in the broadly comic tradition; but the nature of the fable is such that it does not lend itself easily to exploitation as *belles lettres* on a high level." [7] Perry further remarks that many fabulists "prefer to remain anonymous, thinking of themselves only as humble purveyors of children's books or amusing trifles." Aside from the Middle Ages and the late seventeenth and eighteenth centuries, he declares, few of them have regarded their creations as literature.

Perry's estimate sounds more reasonable than Grimm's. At least as far back as all available examples take us, the fable has always been a didactic narrative. To go back farther, as does Grimm, means to speculate; and the nature-oriented prototype that the Romantics come up with simply is not the fable as we know it. Nor, which is more to the point here, does it depict the fable which attracted the didactically-minded eighteenth century.

Furthermore, an honest assessment must conclude, as does Perry, that the fable never has had a rich literary potential. It depends on a rather rigid formula and possesses limited resources for variation and originality. These resources were bound to be exhausted by the multitude of fabulists and dilettantes who applied themselves to the genre during the neoclassic period. In the hands of La Fontaine's eager imitators, out to gain renown as poet-fabulists in their own rights, it often maintained only the slightest contact with the original didactic formula and degenerated into a hackneyed form of light verse—to the disgust of Lessing and others who steadfastly asserted the strict moral purpose of the genre. On the other hand, fabulists who interpreted this purpose as demanding direct, unadorned didacticism operated under conditions of limited possibility for individuality and artistic expression. An inherently restricted literary potential and overwork of this potential by too many poets, most of them second-rate, inevitably resulted in exhaustion. Regarded in this light, it is not surprising that the fable fell from literary favor and returned to its minor but time-honored role of didactic tool and children's literature.

If the fable possesses limited artistic potential, neither would its general specifications seem to allow much room for innovative theories about it. After describing it as a short tale using non-human characters and terminating in a moral lesson, the twentieth-century commentator might not find a whole lot more to say. Thus, in a way it amazes that eighteenth-century essayists, critics, and prefacers did find ample material for original theories and did discover multiple facets on which to expound. Granted, there was much repetition and quibbling, but on the whole less than one would expect. Moreover, much of what might seem quibbling to us did not seem so to them. They took the fable seriously, and they took theory seriously. For the neoclassic man of letters it was important to have a clear theoretical conception of the literary forms with which he dealt, as well as precise definitions of their various parts. Living as we do in the Romantic backwash and under the influence of "progressive" educators, we tend to rely more on individual inspiration and experience; but the orderly eighteenth-century rationalist wanted his destination defined and his route organized before he set out. Pointing out these differences in temperament and training also helps to explain his interest in the fable, which is inherently clear and orderly in both form and purpose.

Aside from dubious literary potential and overwork to explain the demise of the fable as an accepted genre, it could also be claimed that it had served its purpose by the end of the eighteenth century and was no longer needed. Educators and men of letters of the period welcomed the fable as didactic literature. Despite Lessing's protests about poetic perversion and Grimm's claims of didactic perversion, the mainstream of eighteenth-century opinion welcomed the fable precisely because it did combine poetry and didacticism. Didacticism was expected in all literature anyway; and here was a genre which presented its lesson more simply, succinctly, and clearly than any other. These qualities well suited the intense interest in education of the period, which was discussed in Chapter I, and the new literary public forming among the rising middle class. The fable offered unsophisticated literature and a clear but attractively presented lesson. It contained no complexities, subtle nuances, or arcane references. Everybody from eight to eighty and from king to shop clerk could enjoy it and profit from it, an asset remarked time and again by contemporary commentators.

By the end of the century, however, the new middle-class reading public had gained sophistication; and at the same time their world was becoming more complicated, their moral problems no longer lending themselves to capsulization in fables. Reading interests shifted to such forms as the novel and, later, the short story, which were also much better endowed to portray and probe the prevailing social conditions. To give the humble fable credit, however, the short story would be considered an outgrowth of it according to a common neoclassic classification. Gottsched, for example, regards the moral tale using human characters, the ancestor of the short story, as a category of Aesopian fable.

Karl Emmerich, whose depiction of the fable as first rank *Tendenzdichtung* was noted in Chapter I, offers a similar explanation for its decline, although in no way denying its obscurity by the early years of the nineteenth century.[8] He interprets the fabulist's frequent preference for anonymity as due to the potency of the genre as a means of social criticism. The fabulist strikes obliquely, but there is no mistaking his target. Emmerich declares that in the second half of the century the social concern of fables became more pronounced and vigorous until it dominated the traditional moral purpose. Portrayal of increasingly complex human situations resulted in animal characters who tended to be simply masked humans, marking the decline of the genre into a transparent form. The inadequacy of animals to depict and suggest resolutions for complicated social questions became apparent. The result was degeneration of the fable on the one side and abandonment of it on the other in favor of drama and the rapidly developing novel, both of them much more promising mediums for social discussion and propaganda. The fable did its job well, Emmerich concludes, but the combination of inherent limitations and increasing social complexities eventually outmoded it.

In addition to the fondness for didacticism, the classical orientation of seventeenth- and eighteenth-century literary tastes also helps to account for the popularity of the fable. The fable held excellent classical credentials. It also was considered the little brother of the epic, and the histories of the two genres during the neoclassic period follow similar courses.[9] Young writers were expected to imitate classical models in these as in all genres. Just as the budding fabulist adopted Aesop or Phaedrus as guide, the aspiring epic poet followed Homer or Virgil. In retrospect, the fabulists seem to have come up with better results, probably because they chose a less ambitious genre. In any case, both genres died along with exclusively classical tastes; and neither shows signs of revitalization, at least not with its original form and purpose. The eighteenth-century epic poets and their ponderous productions have been accompanied into oblivion by the vast majority of their fabulist contemporaries. Both genres were enthusiastically practiced and discussed at the time; but now both are generally treated as historical literary forms, no longer actively worked.

Epilogue

Although the fable in the nineteenth century no longer ranked among the practiced literary genres, it still received modest critical attention, especially from critics and scholars committed to the classical tradition. In 1858–59 Saint-Marc Girardin delivered a series of lectures at the Sorbonne on *La Fontaine et les fabulistes,* subsequently published in two volumes. As the title indicates, he extols La Fontaine above all other modern fabulists, although generally finding something polite to say about them all; and he pointedly applauds La Fontaine's faithful consultation of classical models before attempting his own creations. Saint-Marc Girardin concludes his lectures with a discussion of contemporary fable writing, which he encourages, and gives the impression of a still viable genre.

Other commentators are not so encouraging. A German educator, writing in 1868, notes that the fable has gone completely out of style in Germany and retains only a pedagogical significance.[1] Another extends the observation to all didactic poetry, which, he claims, since the end of the eighteenth century not only has been excluded from "the realm of the great genres" but has been virtually deprived of all literary rights.[2] Otto Weddigen introduces *Das Wesen und die Theorie der Fabel* (*The Nature and Theory of the Fable,* 1893) with the comment that in his own time the fable "lives only in children's literature as the echo of a style of poetry." [3] Hermann Baumgart dedicates an entire chapter to it in his *Handbuch der Literatur* (*Handbook of Literature,* 1887); but his discussion is historical, most of it concentrated on Lessing's theoretical ideas.

By the early years of the twentieth century fables apparently were losing even the pedagogical significance noted above by the German educator. Jules Arnoux attempts to re-establish interest in them in *La Morale d'après les fables* (1909) and suggests methods for employing them in the classroom, especially to teach morality. An American critic, writing in 1915, remarks the degeneration of the fable into "a plaything for children" and calls it "a *survival,* in the language of the anthropologists, of a form which once occupied the thoughts of mature manhood." [4] More recently, in 1954, an article on the origins of the fable begins by briskly sounding the death knell of the form: "Nowadays the fable is completely out of style for us, even totally dead. To an even greater extent than fairy tales and legends it has disappeared from the last strongholds of its retreat, the schools and playrooms. . . . Once in a while a poet takes an interest in it . . . but hardly otherwise than as a playful imitation or as a joke." [5]

However, there are dissenting opinions. Recent publications, particularly in the German world, suggest that the death knell might have been sounded prematurely. A 1965 Austrian collection of fables, for example, reflects the educational optimism of two centuries ago and shows a high regard for the pedagogical efficacy of the genre. The compiler of the collection, intending it to assist in education both at home and in school, indexes the contents by moral lesson in order to "make possible for the user to find for every desired teaching situation the appropriate fable." [6] In his *Fabeln* (*Fables,* 1970) Klaus Doderer vigorously denies that the form is dead. He points to the fable writing of such well-known twentieth-century authors as Kafka, Brecht, and Thurber and remarks a further post-World War II revival of interest. However, he does admit the virtual omission of the fable from contemporary discussions of literary esthetics.

Notes

CHAPTER ONE: *The Popularity of the Fable and the Rationale*

1. G. Saillard, *Essai sur la fable en France au dix-huitième siècle* (Toulouse & Paris, 1912), p. 30.

2. Erwin Leibfried, *Fabel* (Stuttgart, 1967), p. 67.

3. See Max Plessow, *Geschichte der Fabeldichtung in England bis zu John Gay (1726)*, Palaestra, No. 52 (1906), for a descriptive listing of them.

4. There are several extant German doctoral dissertations on these moral weeklies. See Emil Umbach, *Die deutschen moralischen Wochenschriften und der Spectator von Addison und Steele* (diss. Strasbourg, 1911), p. 60.

5. "An Essay on Fable" in *Selected Fables of Esop, and Other Fabulists* (1761; rpt. London, 1812), p. xliv.

6. Max Staege, *Die Geschichte der deutschen Fabeltheorie, Sprache und Dichtung,* No. 44 (Bern, 1929) is the only work on fable theory that I know of, although limited to German works, as the title indicates. Erwin Leibfried, *Fabel* (Stuttgart, 1967) is an introduction to the genre. Hubert Badstüber, *Die deutsche Fabel: Von ihren ersten Anfängen bis auf die Gegenwart* (Vienna, 1924) gives a short summary of fables and their writers. O. Weddigen, *Das Wesen und die Theorie der Fabel, und ihre Hauptvertreter in Deutschland* (Leipzig, 1893) is worthless, despite the grand title. He gives little more than a summary of Lessing's and Grimm's ideas. Saillard, *Essai sur la Fable en France* . . . gives a good look at the fables and fabulists of the time in France. Saint-Marc Girardin, *La Fontaine et les fabulistes* (Paris, 1867) covers La Fontaine primarily but also other fabulists after him, albeit sketchily—and not always accurately, for foreign ones. Plessow, *Geschichte der Fabeldichtung in England,* covers England as far as John Gay. M. Ellwood Smith, "Notes on the Rimed Fable in England," *MLN,* 31 (1916), 206–16 adds to Plessow's study. Klaus Doderer, *Fabeln* (Zurich, 1970), the most recent comprehensive work on the genre, concentrates on formulating his own ideas but cogently summarizes various other theories in the process.

7. *John Locke on Education,* ed. Peter Gay (New York, 1964), p. 53.

8. London, 1723.

9. See F. Andrew Brown, "On Education: John Locke, Christian Wolff, and the 'Moral Weeklies'," *Univ. of California Pubs. in Modern Philology,* 36, No. 5 (1952), 149–72.

10. In his *Philosophia practica universalis, Pars Posterior* (1739). See Staege, pp. 22–23.

11. *Fables, composée pour l'instruction du Duc de Bourgogne* was written c. 1689 but first published as a collection in 1718.

12. First published 1687, written about 1685.

13. François de Salignac de la Mothe-Fénelon, *Fénelon on Education: A Translation of the "Traité"* . . . *and Other Documents Illustrating Fénelon's Educational Theories and Practice* . . . , ed. H. C. Barnard (Cambridge, 1966), p. 34.

14. Christian Fürchtegott Gellert, *Schriften zur Theorie und Geschichte der Fabel,* ed. Siegfried Scheibe (Tübingen, 1966), p. 17. Translations from foreign-language texts are my own unless otherwise noted.

15. *Der Wolf und das Pferd: Deutsche Tierfabeln des 18. Jahrhunderts,* ed. Karl Emmerich (Berlin, 1960), p. 7.

16. *Veinticinco Siglos de fábulas y apólogos,* ed. Esteban Bagué Nin and Ignacio Bajona Oliveras (Barcelona, 1960), p. 734.

CHAPTER TWO: *La Fontaine and the Seventeenth-Century Forerunners*

1. Charles Hoole, *Aesop's Fables, English and Latin* (London, 1657).

2. *Fables of Aesop and Other Eminent Mythologists* (London, 1692), n. pag.

3. Preface; the following quotation is from the same source.

4. "Dedication" to *The Fables of Aesop Paraphras'd in Verse, and adorn'd with Sculpture* (London, 1651).

5. *Œuvres,* I (Paris, 1883), 14.

6. La Fontaine also remarks on the form and composition of the genre in various of his own fables. Later fabulists often do the same, for example, La Motte, Lichtwer, Gleim, and, of course, Iriarte, all of whose fables concentrate on giving literary advice.

7. *Œuvres,* I, 19 and 16.

8. *Les Fables d'Esope Phrygien* (Brussels, 1669), n. pag.

9. *Fables morales et nouvelles* (Paris, 1671), n. pag.

10. *Traité du poëme epique* (Paris, 1693), p. 4. Page numbers for succeeding references to this work are given in the text.

11. *Fables, Ancient and Modern* (London, 1700), n. pag.

12. London, 1687.

13. Charles Perrault's *Histoires, ou contes* (1697) illustrates a similar duplication of terms. These stories, most of them far exceeding the length normally considered appropriate for the fable, probably best would be called fairy tales or *Märchen;* but all of them include appended moral tags in verse, a characteristic of many fables.

14. *The Critical Works of John Dennis,* ed. E. N. Hooker (Baltimore, 1943), II, 389.

15. "Remarks upon Pope's Homer" (1717), in *Critical Works,* II, 138.

16. *Critical Works,* II, 305.

17. Dennis, *Original Letters* (London, 1721), I, 4. The letter to Blackmore is dated 5 Dec. 1716.

18. *Letters,* I, 6.

19. The original two-volume work started appearing in 1710. It was later expanded to eight volumes.

20. *La Mythologie et les fables* (Paris, 1738), I, 7.

21. Jean Le Rond d'Alembert, "Synonymes," *Œuvres* (Paris, 1822), IV, 252.

22. In the notes to his fables, *Œuvres* (Paris, 1824), IV, 314.

CHAPTER THREE: *Aesop as a Popular Figure and the Fable in England*

1. Bernard Le Bovier de Fontenelle, *Nouveaux Dialogues des morts* (Paris, 1729), p. 24. The dialogue between Aesop and Homer is the fifth one.

2. *Miscellanea. The Second Part* (London, 1692), p. 58.

3. *Works,* ed. Alexander Dyce (London, 1836), II, 223.

4. For an account of the controversy see Anne Elizabeth Burlingame, *The Battle of the Books in Its Historical Setting* (New York, 1920).

5. *Théâtre de Boursault* (Paris, 1746), III, 206.

6. *Aesop. A Comedy* (London, 1697).

7. *Œuvres,* XV–XVI (Paris, 1708).

8. *Œuvres,* XI (Paris, 1708).

9. [Johan de Witt], *Fables Moral and Political* (London, 1703), n. pag.

10. *Aesop at Amsterdam* (Amsterdam, 1698).

11. Preface to *Aesop from Islington* (n. p., 1699).

12. Preface to *Aesop Dress'd* (London, 1705).

13. Preface to *Fables of Aesop, & other Eminent Fabulists.*

14. For additions to L'Estrange's "Reflexions" see [James Gordon, Bishop of Aberdeen], *Remarks on Sir Roger L'Estrange's Edition of Aesop's Fables* (London, 1701). The author seemed to feel that the fables needed even more explanation and illustration, and he wrote this companion volume to L'Estrange's fables.

15. London, 1708, p. x.

16. *Spectator,* No. 183 (29 September 1711).

17. *Spectator,* No. 512 (17 October 1712).

18. Preface to *Fables of Aesop and Others* (London, 1766), n. pag.

19. Gay comments on how hard he worked on the fables of the second volume and intimates Swift's disapproval of the whole fable-writing project in two letters to Swift in 1732. *The Works of Alexander Pope,* ed. Croker and Elwin (London, 1871), vii, 268–69 and 279.

20. *Fables,* ii (London, 1738).

CHAPTER FOUR: *Theories of the Fable: La Motte and Richer*

1. *Fables nouvelles* (Paris, 1719), p. xi. Subsequent references in the text are to this edition.

2. La Motte expresses this idea in his ode "La libre éloquence." The ode itself is in prose.

3. See the "Notes" to *L'Esprit des poésies de M. de la Motte* (Geneva, 1767).

4. Henri Richer, *Fables nouvelles* (Paris, 1748), p. ix.

CHAPTER FIVE: *The Fable in Germany During the First Half-Century*

1. Foreword to *Versuch in poetischen Fabeln und Erzählungen* (Hamburg, 1738).

2. *Versuch einer critischen Dichtkunst für die Deutschen* (Darmstadt, 1962), p. 161. A facsimile rpt. of the Leipzig, 1751, 4th ed.

3. "Vorbericht" to *Moralische Fabeln*, printed as a "Poetischer Anhang" in *Poetischer Betrachtungen*, II (Hamburg, 1746), 593. This "Vorbericht" is the same one used to introduce the 1737 edition of fables, plus later remarks added in footnotes.

4. "Vorbericht" to *Neue äsopische Fabeln* (Hamburg, 1740).

5. *Critische Dichtkunst* (Stuttgart, 1966), I, 166. A facsimile rpt. of the 1740 ed.

6. See Max Staege, *Die Geschichte der deutschen Fabeltheorie*, p. 31.

7. Georg Friedrich Meier and Samuel G. Lange, *Der Gesellige: Eine moralische Wochenschrift* (Halle, 1764), I, 742.

8. "Critische Vorrede" to *Ein halbes Hundert neuer Fabeln* (Zurich, 1744), n. pag.

9. *Kritische Briefe* (Zurich, 1746), p. 164.

10. *The Idler*, original No. 22, 16 September 1758. Johnson replaced it with a tamer piece in the collected edition. The fable was reprinted in several other journals of the time. There seems no good reason to doubt that Johnson was capable of such misanthropy and every reason to believe that he himself wrote it. See *The Idler and the Adventurer*, ed. Bate, Bullitt & Powell (New Haven & London, 1963), *The Yale Edition of the Works of Samuel Johnson*, II.

11. Preface to *Fables for the Female Sex* (London 1744).

12. *Kritische Briefe*, p. 195.

13. Gleim, *Sämtliche Schriften* (Reutlingen, 1779), p. 8.

14. *Schriften zur Theorie und Geschichte der Fabel*, ed. Siegfried Scheibe (Tübingen, 1966), p. 121. The edition has the Latin original and the German translation on facing pages.

15. Friedrich der Grosse, *De la Littérature allemande (1780)*, ed. Ludwig Geiger (Berlin, 1902), p. 6. Later in the discussion Frederick gives the German interest in Shakespeare as an example of his countrymen's bad taste: Shakespeare was acceptable in his own country and own time when people did not know any better, but there is no excuse for Goethe's *Götz von Berlichingen*, a contemporary imitation of Shakespeare (pp. 23 f.).

16. *Schriften zur Theorie und Geschichte der Fabel*, p. 11.

CHAPTER SIX: *French Ideas at Mid-Century*

1. *Principes de la littérature*, 2 vols. (Paris, 1764), I, 294–95.

2. *Principes de la littérature*, II, 1.

3. Marmontel, *Œuvres* (Paris, 1787), VII, 370.

4. "Avant-Propos" to *Fables et œuvres diverses* (Paris, 1774), I, v.

5. Melchior Grimm provides a contemporary opinion of Aubert's own fables: "Vous y en trouverez de fort jolies, et dans celles qui ne sont pas bonnes il y a toujours quelques jolis morceaux. Cela est bien loin du génie, de la grâce et de la naïveté de La Fontaine; mais il est vrai aussi que M. l'abbé Aubert est très-supérieur a tous ses confrères les fabulistes d'aujourd'hui." *Correspondance littéraire,* IV, 418–19.

CHAPTER SEVEN: *Lessing's Aesopian Fables and the Anti-Lessing*

1. *Fabeln: Drei Bücher,* in *Lessings Werke, in fünf Bänden* (Berlin and Weimar, 1964), V, 110–11. Hereafter references to volume and page no. in *Lessings Werke* will appear in my text.

2. Hans Lothar Markschies, "Lessing und die asopische Fabel," *Wissenschaftliche Zeitschrift der Karl-Marx-Universität Leipzig. Gesellschafts-und Sprachwissenschaftliche Reihe,* IV (1954–55), No. 1–2, pp. 134 ff.

3. See, e.g., Hermann Baumgart, *Handbuch der Poetik* (Stuttgart, 1887), and Otto Weddigen, *Das Wesen und die Theorie der Fabel, und ihre Hauptvertreter in Deutschland* (Leipzig, 1893).

4. Markschies, p. 136: "So beobachtet Lessing die Literatur seines Jahrhunderts, skeptisch gegen ihre Art von Poesie, die die Wahrheit versäumt. Dem Leser aber wird es überlassen, den Schlusz aus solcher Erkenntnis zu ziehen: *dasz mit der Fabeltheorie zugleich die ganze Dichtung erneuert werden soll."* His italics.

5. See, e.g., Adolf Laun, "Über Yriartes literarische Fabeln," in *Programm des Gymnasiums zu Oldenburg zum Oster-Examen 1868* (Oldenburg, 1868), p. 1: "Bekanntlich giebt es für die Fabel zwei entgegengesetzte Systeme, die ich der Kürze wegen das Lessingsche und das Lafontainsche nennen will."

6. *Correspondance littéraire . . . ,* ed. Maurice Tourneux (Paris, 1877), VI, 141.

7. Letter of July 1773, X, 265.

8. VII, 35–55.

9. *Lessingsche unäsopische Fabeln* (Zurich, 1760), p. 6.

10. *Lessingsche unäsopische Fabeln,* p. 192.

11. In Bodmer's *Kritische Briefe,* discussed in Chapter V above. For Lessing's reply to Bodmer see *Briefe, die neueste Literatur betreffend,* No. 127 (18 Sept. 1760 and 25 September 1760).

12. X (1760), 748–57.

13. Bodmer, *Schriften, ausgewählt von Fritz Ernst* (Zurich, 1938), p. 73.

CHAPTER EIGHT: *Rousseau and the Fable in Education*

1. See Ch. II, pp. 14 ff.

2. Ch. III, pp. 33 ff.

3. *Remarks on Sir Roger L'Estrange's Edition of Aesop's Fables* (London, 1701).

4. Jean Baptiste Morvan de Bellegarde, *Les Fables d'Esope Phrigien, avec celles de Philelphe* (Utrecht, 1729), 2 vols.

5. "Vorrede" to *Aesopus des Phrygiers Leben und Fabeln . . . mit des Herrn Abts von Bellegarde moralischen und historischen Anmerkungen* (Copenhagen & Leipzig, 1781), p. vii.

6. Zurich, 1748, p. 105.

7. The discussion is found in Book V of *Julie.*

8. The discussion of fables comes from Book II of *Émile,* which concerns education from ages five to twelve.

9. *Émile, Œuvres complètes,* ed. Gagnebin and Raymond (Dijon, 1969), IV, 352.

10. Henry Home, Lord Kames, *Introduction to the Art of Thinking* (New York, 1818), pp. v–vi.

11. *Correspondance littéraire,* V, 172.

12. "Avant-Propos" to his own fables, in *Fables et œuvres diverses,* I.

13. *Fables et œuvres diverses,* I, 311. The "Discours" appeared with the original 1756 edition but was revised for the enlarged 1764 edition.

14. *Über die wirksamsten Mittel Kindern Religion beyzubringen* (Leipzig, 1787), pp. 55–56.

15. *Lesebuch für Kinder* (Munich, 1778), "Vorrede."

16. *Zweckmässige Fabeln* (Berlin, 1805), "Vorrede."

17. *Entwurf* (Berlin & Stettin, 1783), p. 56.

CHAPTER NINE: *Dodsley and England at Mid-Century*

1. Preface, *Aesop's Fables* (London, 1753), p. xii.

2. See *Hrn. Samuel Richardsons Sittenlehre für die Jugend in der auserlesensten Aesopischen Fabeln* (Leipzig, 1783). Klaus Doderer states that this German translation first appeared in 1757 without Lessing's name as translator. *Fabeln* (Zurich, 1970), p. 234.

3. Preface to *Selected Fables of Esop, and other Fabulists* (London, 1812). Edwin Pearson, writing in the preface to *Bewick's Select Fables* (London, 1879), says that the "distinguished gentlemen" who contributed to the original fables were probably Samuel Johnson and Oliver Goldsmith. The "learned friend" he suggests to have been Goldsmith (pp. xxv ff.).

4. "A New Life of Aesop," *Selected Fables of Esop . . .*, pp. xvi, xxv.

5. William Shenstone, a friend of Dodsley's, advised him in the fable project. In a letter of 24 April 1750 to a certain John Scott Hylton, Shenstone writes: "La Motte has lately afforded me not a little entertainment: I read it on acct. of Dodsley, who you know is writing *Fables*, & ask'd my Thoughts upon the *subject*." *The Letters of William Shenstone*, ed. Marjorie Williams (Oxford, 1939), p. 514.

6. "An Essay on Fable," *Selected Fables of Esop . . .*, p. xxxvi. The essay has been reprinted by the Augustan Reprint Society (Publ. No. 112): Dodsley, *An Essay on Fable*, introd. Jeanne K. Welcher & Richard Dircks (Los Angeles, 1965).

7. E.g., La Motte, Triller, Breitinger. To round out opinion on the lion-maiden romance, there is the positive comment in [James Gordon, Bishop of Aberdeen], *Remarks on Sir Roger L'Estrange's Edition of Aesop's Fables:* good people fall in love with animals; and besides, love softens all, including lions. (Commentary to L'Estrange's fable No. 121)

8. *Monthly Review*, 24 (March 1761), 150.

9. Robert Anderson, ed. *The Works of the British Poets* (London, 1795), XI, 80.

10. *The Art of Poetry on a New Plan* (London, 1762), I, 245–46.

11. Goldsmith is credited with the authorship by Edwin Pearson in a preface to the 1879 edition: *Bewick's Select Fables, of Aesop and Others* (London, 1879). Pearson claims that Goldsmith wrote many prefaces and essays during this period and that this "Essay on Fable" reflects his style. *CBEL* quotes Pearson but finds no other evidence of Goldsmith's authorship. Such recent works as Ralph M. Wardle's biography, *Oliver Goldsmith* (Lawrence, Kan., 1957), and Arthur Friedman's *Collected Works of Oliver Goldsmith* (Oxford, 1966) make no mention of the essay nor of any connection between Goldsmith and *Bewick's Select Fables*. See above for Pearson's allegations that Goldsmith contributed to Dodsley's volume.

12. *Bewick's Select Fables* (London, 1879), p. xxxvii.

13. *Dissertations Moral and Critical* (London, 1783), p. 506.

14. Advertisement to *Fables Moral and Sentimental* (London, 1772).

CHAPTER TEN: *Herder and the Romantic Turn*

1. *Allgemeine Theorie der schönen Künste* (Leipzig, 1792), II, 164. Sulzer also includes an article on *Fabel (Dichtkunst)*—as opposed to *Fabel (Die Aesopische)*—which he defines as the plot or events that make up the material of epic or drama.

2. Hamann, *Schriften,* ed. Friedrich Roth (Berlin, 1821–43), III, 19.

3. Letter to J. G. Lindner (5 May 1761), *Schriften,* III, 82.

4. Letter to Herder (28 December 1767), *Schriften,* III, 378.

5. In *Über die neuere Deutsche Literatur. Fragmente, als Beilagen zu den Briefen, die neueste Literatur betreffend. Dritte Sammlung* (Riga, 1767), *Sämtliche Werke,* ed. Bernhard Suphan (Berlin, 1877–1913), I, 434.

6. *Sämtliche Werke,* II, 189. Hereafter reference to volume and page will appear in the text.

7. *Zerstreute Blätter* (Gotha, 1786), Zweite Sammlung, *Sämtliche Werke,* XV, 490.

8. Goethe, *Werke,* ed. Gustav von Loeper, et al. (Weimar, 1887–1919), XXXVII, 219.

9. Friedrich von Hardenberg, *Fragmente,* ed. Ernst Kamnitzer (Dresden, 1929), p. 667. The comments on the fable appear in fragments numb. 2065 and 2066.

10. *Œuvres* (Paris, 1776), III, 121.

11. Voltaire, in the article "Fable" in his *Dictionnaire Philosophique,* also remarks a rebellious aspect of the fable, declaring that it was invented in Asia by subjugated people; free people have no need to disguise the truth. But he also points out that all men— subjugated or free—love stories and images. Most of his discussion concerns La Fontaine's position in the age of Louis XIV (prominent) and his style (faulty).

12. *Fables, contes et épitres* (Paris, 1773), p. iii.

13. Melchior Grimm derides Le Monnier's claim that the fable cannot be defined: "On dirait presque que M. l'abbé Le M. n'a eu d'autre but dans son discours que celui de persuader à ses lecteurs qu'il a fait ses fables . . . sans le savoir. . . . . La prétention au génie est la manie de ce siècle. Autrefois on se contenait à moins, et l'on ne prétendait qu'à l'esprit." *Correspondance Littéraire,* ed. Maurice Tourneux (Paris, 1877), X, 267.

14. *Œuvres complètes* (Leipzig, 1796), VIII, 195.

CHAPTER ELEVEN: *Samaniego, Iriarte, and the Fable in Spain*

1. *Fábulas en verso castellano* (Madrid, 1796), pp. viii–ix.

2. See "Advertencia del editor, puesta al frente de la primera impresión de 1782," in *Fábulas literarias, Colección de obras en verso y prosa de D. Tomás de Yriarte,* I (Madrid, 1787).

3. For a study of Iriarte's neoclassicism see Manfred Lentzen, "Tomas de Iriartes Fabeln und der Neoklassizmus in Spanien," *Romanische Forschungen,* 79, No. 4 (1967), 603–20.

4. "Literarische Fabeln: aus dem Spanischen des Don Tomas de Iriarte," *Der deutsche Merkur,* 46 (1784), 86.

5. "De la Fable," *Œuvres complètes* (Leipzig, 1796), VIII, 193.

6. See Russell P. Sebold, *Tomás de Iriarte: Poeta de "Rapto Racional"* (Oviedo, 1961), p. 11.

7. *El Asno erudito,* ed. Manuel Muñoz Cortés (Valencia, 1948), pp. 56–57.

8. See Muñoz Cortés's introduction to his edition of *El Asno erudito* for a characterization of the two and a cogent summary of the ensuing stratagems by both sides.

A different interpretation comes from Rafael Bosch and Ronald Cere, *Los Fabulistas y su sentido histórico* (New York: Colección Iberia, 1969), which emphasizes the underlying political concern of both Iriarte and Samaniego. According to this interpretation Iriarte's ultimate concern in his "literary fables" was not literary at all but political and satirical: "Pero aquí pretendemos convencer al lector de que la mayor parte de las fábulas de Iriarte no son literarias, y que se llaman así para evitar la suspicacia del ignorante, aunque serían leídas y recitadas por los entusiastas de su crítica política con perfecto conocimiento de las circunstancias que se comentaban y con perfecta consciencia de las personas a quienes se dirigía la sátira, ya fueran individuos o tipos" (p. 21). Samaniego emerges as equally oriented to political and social matters, even though he originally composed his fables for the use of schoolboys. Forner, according to this interpretation, headed the forces of reaction—"era el elemento más reaccionario de toda la literatura del reinado de Carlos III" (p. 24). He composed his *Asno erudito* specifically to counteract Iriarte's liberal views.

Others have noted subtle satire of contemporary figures in Iriarte's fables—see, for example, Emilio Cotarelo y Mori's *Iriarte y su época* (Madrid, 1897)—but this study by Bosch and Cere emphasizes the political and social concern of the Spanish fabulists to the virtual exclusion of all others. Both authors (Cere is Bosch's student) are advocates of the socio-historical approach to literary criticism and seek to demonstrate "la fundamentación histórico-social de la literatura" (p. 9).

9. In *Obras inéditas ó poco conocidas* (Vitoria, 1866). "Observaciones" was published with neither place nor date of publication, but the editors of this edition declare the date to have been 1782.

10. *Obras inéditas,* p. 131.

11. See the introduction to *Obras inéditas,* pp. 62 f.

CHAPTER TWELVE: *Dissolution of a Functioning Literary Genre*

1. *Sämtliche Werke,* XXIII, 253.

2. *Werke,* XXVII, 79. The comment is in Book VII of the second part of *Dichtung und Wahrheit.*

3. *Œuvres*, IV, v. Arnault's explicit equation of "fable" and "apologue" was mentioned at the end of Chapter II. He also discusses the etymology of "fable," tracing it to a root meaning *parler* and noting its Latin designation of *conte* or *récit*. However, "l'usage a donné à ces deux mots des valeurs très distinctes. Le conte est un récit inventé dans le but de divertir; et quand par hasard le conte est moral, on a grand soin de l'annoncer par le titre, ce qui prouve que le conte moral est une exception dans le genre. La fable, au contraire, est un récit fait dans l'intention d'instruire. La fable doit offrir une moralité: celle qui s'ecartent de cette régle rentrent dans la classe des contes." *Œuvres*, IV, 315–16.

4. In *Critiques philosophiques et littéraires, Œuvres,* VI, 425.

5. In *Estudios de literatura, española y comparada* (Santa Cruz de Tenerife, 1951).

6. See Otto Crusius, "Aus der Geschichte der Fabel," introd. to *Das Buch der Fabeln,* ed. C. H. Kleukens (Leipzig, 1920), p. xxxv.

7. "Fable," *Studium Generale,* 12, No. 1 (1959), 29.

8. "Vorwort" to *Der Wolf und das Pferd: Deutsche Tierfabeln des 18. Jahrhunderts* (Berlin, 1960).

9. Grimm notes this parallel in his "Essence of the Animal Fable" cited above.

EPILOGUE

1. Adolf Laun, "Über Yriartes literarische Fabeln," in *Programm des Gymnasiums zu Oldenburg zum Oster-Examen 1868* (Oldenburg, 1868).

2. Gustav Diestel, "Bausteine zur Geschichte der deutschen Fabel," in *Program des Vitzhumschen Gymnasiums* (Dresden, 1871), p. 5.

3. Leipzig, 1893, p. 5.

4. M. Ellwood Smith, "The Fable and Kindred Forms," *JEGP,* 14 (1915), 519.

5. Karl Meuli, "Herkunft und Wesen der Fabel," *Schweizerisches Archiv für Volkskunde,* 50, No. 2 (1954), 65.

6. Erwin Heinzel, "Vorwort" to *Kleines Fabel-ABC* (Vienna, 1965).

Bibliography

Listed are works which treat or touch on theories of the fable in the eighteenth century. Such works are few, and of those listed below only Staege's is dedicated entirely to the subject. Critical treatments of fabulists or collections of fables, especially of La Fontaine and Aesop, abound but have only a peripheral bearing on the subject at hand.

Badstüber, Hubert. *Die deutsche Fabel: Von ihren ersten Anfängen bis auf die Gegenwart.* Vienna, 1924.

Bagué Nin, Esteban, and Ignacio Bajona Oliveras. Introd. to *Veinticinco Siglos de fábulas y apólogos.* Barcelona, 1960.

Cioranescu, Alejandro. *Estudios de literatura, española y comparada.* Santa Cruz de Tenerife, 1951.

Crusius, Otto. "Aus der Geschichte der Fabel." Introd. to *Das Buch der Fabeln.* Ed. C. H. Kleukens. Leipzig, 1920.

Doderer, Klaus. *Fabeln: Formen, Figuren, Lehren.* Zurich, 1970.

Leibfried, Erwin. *Fabel.* Stuttgart, 1967.

Perry, Ben Edwin. "Fable." *Studium Generale,* 12, No. 1 (1959), 17–37.

Plessow, Max. *Geschichte der Fabeldichtung in England bis zu John Gay.* Palaestra, No. 52 (1906).

Saillard, G. *Essai sur la fable en France au dix-huitiéme siècle.* Toulouse & Paris, 1912.

Saint-Marc Girardin, François Auguste. *La Fontaine et les fabulistes.* 2 vols. Paris, 1867.

Staege, Max. *Die Geschichte der deutschen Fabeltheorie. Sprache und Dichtung,* No. 44. Bern, 1929.

Weddigen, Otto. *Das Wesen und die Theorie der Fabel, und ihre Hauptvertreter in Deutschland.* Leipzig, 1893.

Index

Addison, Joseph, 23, 35, 36, 40, 77, 124, 159

Aesop, 2, 16, 33, 36, 53, 112, 120, 133, 140, 152; popularity and utility of his fables, 1, 7, 10, 47, 102, 103; compared with other fabulists, 3, 13, 18, 39, 41, 44, 62, 67, 74, 80, 109, 126-28, 137, 149; his life, 4, 25, 40, 114-15, 124; as a guide to fable writing, 5, 42, 49, 55, 57, 61, 70, 79, 87, 93-97, 99, 138, 156; editions of his fables, 8, 15, 103, 114-15; his fables compared with fables of other genres, 19, 21-22, 24, 82; as a literary character, 26-29, 30-32

Aldrich, Henry, Dean of Oxford, 26

Alembert, Jean le Rond d', 23

Allegory, 65; as a characteristic of fables, 19, 21, 39, 43-44, 45, 56, 57, 76, 79, 80, 93, 97, 98-99, 100, 115-16, 118-19, 127, 131, 136, 138; as a teaching device, 33; differentiated from fable, 75, 87, 88-89, 91, 95; origins of, 77, 124, 129

Ancients-Moderns controversy, 26-27, 38, 39, 41

Anderson, Robert, 118

Aphthonius, 92

"Apologue" (meaning discussed), 16-17, 23, 169

Aristotle, 94, 127, 128

Arnault, Antoine, 23, 147-48, 149, 169

Arnoux, Jules, 158

Art of Poetry on a New Plan, The, 118

Arwaker, Edmund, 33-35, 102

Aubert, Abbé Jean-Louis, 74, 82-84, 109-10, 145, 164

Bacon, Francis, 6

Badstüber, Hubert, 159

Bagué Nin, Esteban, 160

Bajona Oliveras, Ignacio, 160

Banier, Antoine, 22-23

Batteux, Charles, 79, 92, 124, 149, 150; *Beaux Arts réduits,* 74-76; *Cours de belles-lettres,* 74, 76-78; Lessing's criticism of, 88-91

Battle of the Books, 2, 161

Baudoin, J., 17, 29

Baumgart, Hermann, 157, 164

Bayle, Pierre, 23, 25

Beattie, James, 119-20

Bellegarde, Abbé Jean Baptiste Morvan de, 103

Belustigungen des Verstandes und des Witzes, 59, 67, 72

Bentley, Dr. Richard, 26-27

Bewick's Select Fables, 119, 166

Bibliothek der schönen Wissenschaften und freyen Kunst, 3, 97

Blackmore, Sir Richard, 21

Boccaccio, Giovanni, 20, 68

Bodmer, Johann Jakob, 50-51, 54, 59, 69, 73, 101, 103, 122, 133; "Critical Introduction," 60-62, 66-67; *Kritische Briefe,* 62-66; *Lessingsche unäsopische Fabeln,* 97-100, 128